THE
DEADLY
SEA

THE DEADLY SEA

Life and Death on the Atlantic

JIM WELLMAN

FLANKER PRESS LIMITED
ST. JOHN'S

Library and Archives Canada Cataloguing in Publication

Wellman, Jim, 1946-, author
    The deadly sea : life and death on the Atlantic / Jim Wellman.

Includes index.
Issued in print and electronic formats.
ISBN 978-1-77117-397-1 (pbk.).--ISBN 978-1-77117-398-8 (epub).--
ISBN 978-1-77117-399-5 (Kindle).--ISBN 978-1-77117-400-8 (pdf)

    1. Seafaring life--Atlantic Provinces--Anecdotes. 2. Fishers--
Atlantic Provinces--Anecdotes. 3. Fisheries--Atlantic Provinces--
Anecdotes. 4. Atlantic Provinces--Anecdotes. I. Title.

FC2019.S42W45 2015   971.5   C2015-902659-8
                    C2015-902660-1

© 2015 Jim Wellman

PRINTED IN CANADA

This paper has been certified to meet the environmental and social standards of the Forest Stewardship Council® (FSC®) and comes from responsibly managed forests, and verified recycled sources.

Cover Design by Graham Blair

FLANKER PRESS LTD.
PO BOX 2522, STATION C
ST. JOHN'S, NL
CANADA

TELEPHONE: (709) 739-4477 FAX: (709) 739-4420 TOLL-FREE: 1-866-739-4420
WWW.FLANKERPRESS.COM

9 8 7 6 5 4 3 2 1

We acknowledge the financial support of the Government of Canada through the Canada Book Fund (CBF) and the Government of Newfoundland and Labrador, Department of Tourism, Culture and Recreation for our publishing activities. We acknowledge the support of the Canada Council for the Arts, which last year invested $153 million to bring the arts to Canadians throughout the country. *Nous remercions le Conseil des arts du Canada de son soutien. L'an dernier, le Conseil a investi 153 millions de dollars pour mettre de l'art dans la vie des Canadiennes et des Canadiens de tout le pays.*

CONTENTS

DEDICATION AND ACKNOWLEDGEMENTS

A friend once said he thought that what I write about is very important.

I asked what he meant.

"It is extremely important that the stories of tragedy, rescue, courage, and bravery of our inshore fishing people be kept alive through stories like those you write. Otherwise, they would soon be forgotten and lost forever to everyone but the immediate family, and that would be a sad and terrible thing," he said.

I reflected on his words, especially about the brave and courageous.

He was right.

People use the word "hero" a little lightly these days. It's hardly heroism when someone rescues a kitten from a tree when, if left alone, the animal would likely have figured out the route to safety all by itself.

In some of the chapters you will meet some real heroes—ones who deserve great recognition and even medals of honour.

My friend's words made me realize that it's important to shine a light on some of the other very interesting people in the fishing industry: the people who build boats, who operate fish plants, and people like the two women you will meet in Chapter 4—they sell fish: fresh, frozen, or cooked—they are all important cogs in the survival wheel of the industry that was and still is, in many rural areas, the backbone of our economy and our culture.

This book is dedicated to all of them.

Once again, I'd like to thank the publishers of the *Navigator Magazine* for their continued support of my work by carrying these articles in their publication. Paul Pinhorn, Trevor Decker, and Rick Young have not only supported me but have constantly offered their encouragement to keep telling the stories of the amazing people in the fishing industry in all of Atlantic Canada.

And, of course, I want to express my heartfelt gratitude to all of the people who allowed me to invade their privacy by asking them very personal and often painful questions about loved ones lost at sea. I have boundless respect for all of you.

Thank you all.

Jim Wellman
St. John's, 2015

THE
DEADLY
SEA

CHAPTER 1

Family Vacation Turns Tragic

Loyola Pomroy was vacationing with his family at home in Placentia, Newfoundland, in July 1972. Loyola grew up on Merasheen Island but left home in 1965 to attend Memorial University in St. John's. He later got a job at a bank and in 1970 was transferred to Halifax, Nova Scotia.

Two years after Loyola left home, his parents moved from Merasheen to live in Placentia as part of the government's resettlement program, but his dad, Leo Pomroy, along with Leo's brother Pat, returned to the island every summer to fish. Merasheen was about a two-and-a-half-hour boat ride from Placentia, so Leo and Pat would go home to Placentia on Saturday evening to spend the weekend with their families and return to Merasheen on Monday morning.

Having lived in Halifax for two years, Loyola couldn't wait to include a visit to Merasheen as part of his summer vacation in 1972. While planning a few days on the island, he thought how extra special it would be if his mom, his three younger sisters, and six-year-old brother could be there, too. It would be like a homecoming for the family. After some discussion, everyone grew more and more excited about the trip, and soon the list of family members grew to include an aunt, a cousin, a brother-in-law, and Loyola's girlfriend (now wife), Judy Snow.

Loyola Pomroy

Loyola arranged passage for the group to get to Merasheen on board the *Bertha Joyce*, a fish collector based in nearby Arnold's Cove. National Sea Products operated a fish plant in Arnold's Cove and had vessels that travelled to various fishing communities around Placentia Bay, including Merasheen, to collect fish from fishing crews and bring it back to the plant for processing. With no cold storage facilities in most of the communities, the collector boats made return trips several times a week. Local fishermen and their family members often took advantage of the collectors to hitch a ride between communities.

On Monday, July 24, the Pomroy clan arrived at Arnold's Cove bright and early to join Captain Ray Berkshire, on board the schooner *Bertha Joyce*, for the trip across Placentia Bay to Merasheen, where they would spend three or four days roaming the meadows and cliffs of their beloved island. For Loyola it was another opportunity to spend a few mornings fishing in the trap skiff that he had spent many summer days working in with his dad during his teenage years. It was a great joy to live life to the fullest back on the old homestead, away from the city and all the trappings that go hand in hand with the city lifestyle.

The family had a wonderful time enjoying the freedom of the open spaces of a twenty-mile-long island located in the middle of Placentia Bay, but all too soon it was time to go back home to Placentia.

Captain Berkshire notified Loyola that, due to the collector boat's schedules on Thursday, he would not be able to accommodate the family that day on the *Bertha Joyce*, but he would arrange with Captain Reuben Evans for them to join National Sea's other collector vessel, *Delroy*, which would be leaving Merasheen for Arnold's Cove on Thursday evening.

The evening weather on Thursday was about as good as it gets in Placentia Bay. The south coast of Newfoundland is renowned for fog in prevailing south and southwest winds at that time of year, but on July 27, 1972, seas were moderate with clear skies. The full moon allowed for excellent visibility even after dark, so, all in all, it would be a perfect evening for a boat trip across Placentia Bay.

Captain Evans and the crew of the *Delroy* had been collecting fish all day in various Placentia Bay communities and made Merasheen the last port of call, perhaps in consideration of the Pomroy family, so that their home port in Arnold's Cove would be the next stop. Just as the *Delroy* finished loading fish Thursday evening, the ten-member Pomroy clan boarded the vessel and settled in for the four-hour journey to Arnold's Cove.

As the *Delroy* pulled away from the shores of Merasheen, the Pomroy family gazed back for a last glance at the rocky shores of Merasheen and waved goodbye to the Pomroy brothers Leo and Pat standing on the wharf. Pat's wife, Nellie, was one of the group waving to her husband from the deck of the *Delroy*. It was approximately 9:00 p.m. and getting dark, so the passengers began looking for a place to get comfortable for the next four hours. The *Delroy* was an eighty-foot schooner, built for work in the fishing industry, and not designed for passengers, so comfortable seating for ten passengers and five crew members was at a premium.

It was a fine July evening, so some stayed on deck for a while, but most of them found a place to sit in a cabin located just behind the wheelhouse, at the stern section of the vessel, directly above the engine room. A few of the adults played cards while Jean Pomroy, Loyola's mother, kept a close eye on her children, especially six-year-old Billy. Loyola and his brother-in-law, Ernie Pitcher, chatted with a couple of the crew before joining the rest of the family in the cabin. Loyola sat on a bunk with his back against a wall and eventually drifted off to sleep.

"The next thing I remember, my mother was calling me, saying there was a smell of smoke in the cabin, so I jumped up and ran out on the deck to see what was going on," he says.

Once outside, Loyola realized that whatever was happening must have been serious, because one or two of the crew, along with Ernie, were quickly removing things from a dory, situated on the starboard deck in front of the wheelhouse, and preparing it for use as a lifeboat.

"They were throwing stuff out of the dory as fast as they could. Some of it was landing on the deck and some of it was going overboard," Loyola remembers.

Still uncertain of exactly what was happening, Loyola ran back into the cabin just in time to see the engineer, Leo Bullen, grab a fire extinguisher and open the hatch door leading down to the engine room. That was when the situation went from serious to critical. As soon as the hatch door opened, flames came licking up through the hatch opening.

"I suppose it was the intense heat, but whatever it was, I saw the engineer throw the fire extinguisher through the hatch opening down into the engine room. He just threw it!" Loyola recalls.

With that scene playing out in front of his eyes, and then the sound of two or three explosions, it became obvious that it was time to get everyone off the burning vessel, and the quicker the better. But, as Loyola Pomroy soon discovered, much to his dismay, getting off the *Delroy* to safety was not going to be an easy task, if it was possible at all.

Delroy (Photo courtesy of Mac MacKay)

The entire wheelhouse and cabin were aflame as Loyola and others worked feverishly to prepare the only lifeboat on board the *Delroy*. The only lifeboat was actually a dory—it was designed as a work boat and not a real life-saving boat. However, the dory was large, about twenty feet long, and could possibly hold fifteen people—a bonus considering that three of them would be children—but only if everyone could get on board the boat in an orderly fashion. With fire spreading quickly, now just a few feet from the dory on the deck, time was running out. It was too hot, and too risky for anyone to enter the wheelhouse and stop the engine, so the *Delroy* was left to steam along at approximately eight nautical miles an hour. With people in various stages of panic, scrambling from the burning vessel into a dory while the vessel was moving was not going to happen in an orderly manner. Meanwhile, the large dory was very heavy, and it took a lot of precious time to get it over the side and into the water.

Delroy (Photo courtesy of Mac MacKay)

Loyola jumped from the schooner into the dory, with the intention of having Ernie pass down the smaller children to him first, and then help the remaining family members over the side and, presumably, the captain and crew would follow. Despite the fear and confusion, fourteen people made it from the deck into the dory, while one crewman, Engineer Leo Bullen, stayed back to untie the dory from the burning schooner.

Loyola explains that after forty-two years his memory of some details of the unfolding events at that time have faded, but he does recall the scene as the engineer let go the painter (bow rope) of the dory and then ran to jump over the *Delroy*'s rail into the lifeboat.

"It was like slow motion. He let go the painter, and when he did the dory suddenly slowed down, so he had to run back from the bow to the stern to catch up and get ready to jump."

Loyola is not certain whether the engineer actually landed in the dory or not. He doesn't think so because, at the very instant Leo jumped, the dory's stabilizing forces changed. The small boat was no longer attached to the *Delroy* and was now free-floating. The dory was probably capable of carrying fifteen people under normal circumstances, if all had been appropriately placed to distribute the total weight from bow to stern, but there was nothing normal about that night. It's possible that too many people had congregated to one side. Seconds after Leo untied the dory, it capsized, throwing all hands overboard.

At twenty-four, Loyola Pomroy was in the best physical condition of his entire life. A natural athlete, Loyola loved sports. In Halifax, where he was living at the time, he played hockey eight times a week, once every day and twice on Saturdays. His strength and good condition, combined with the fact that he was a good swimmer, contributed to the survival of six people that night. His physical and emotional strength would be tested to the limit.

Developing a rescue strategy that required making the most of every minute was crucial. With a mixture of men, women, and children, all but one without flotation devices of any kind, and nothing but an overturned flat-bottomed boat to try and cling to, survival would be almost impossible for some, if not all of them. Added to the challenge was the frigid water. Although July is usually the warmest time of year in Newfoundland, the northwest Atlantic Ocean was experiencing a wide-ranging cold period in 1972, and Placentia Bay temperatures hovered at just about three or four degrees above freezing. Besides the initial shock to the body when suddenly immersed in near-freezing water, one's senses quickly become numb as the body temperature drops significantly. Decisions must be made before hypothermia advances to the stage where rational thinking is compromised.

Despite the odds, Loyola remained calm and took the leadership role in developing a survival plan. Herding those who surfaced near the dory to both sides of the overturned boat, he had them reach across the bottom of the dory and grip each other's hands. The closest two were his sister Carmel and his fiancée, Judy Snow. Captain Evans and his son, Clarence, climbed onto the bottom of the dory and tried to assist the other crew members in the water. Leo Bullen and one other crewman were soon alongside the dory. Because he was the last to leave the *Delroy*, Leo had the only life jacket that anyone could remember seeing. It was old-fashioned, with flotation material in the front and back joined by straps.

"The crew members were doing their own thing and I was trying to do whatever I could for our family," Loyola says.

As soon as Carmel and Judy were safe, Loyola started searching for the others. It was dark, and although it was relatively calm, a small lop on the dark water made it difficult to see anyone, even just a few feet away.

"I sort of thought that I wouldn't find anyone alive at this point, especially the children, because they couldn't swim or anything," he says.

After what Loyola thinks may have been about four or five minutes swimming, he saw what appeared to be a black object that at first caused him some alarm.

"I recall thinking that it could be a shark," he says.

Despite his fear, he swam toward the object and was elated to find it was his cousin, thirteen-year-old Marjorie Ennis, and she was alive, barely. Although she couldn't swim, Marjorie managed to tread water, and despite having gone under twice or more, she kept her head above the surface most of the time and hoped for the best.

Loyola swam his cousin back to the others at the dory and then set out to search for more family members, hopeful that, like Marjorie, some of them had held on long enough to be found alive.

But fate had other plans, and Loyola would soon be facing an emotional reality almost beyond comprehension.

After getting his cousin Marjorie situated safely at the side of the overturned dory, along with Carmel and Judy, Loyola swam back to where he had found Marjorie, hoping there were others in the same area. For several minutes he scanned the surface of the dark ocean, hoping to see something, all the while calling out and listening for a response. But there was nothing but darkness and silence. At length he saw something in the distance, but it looked too large to be a person. Swimming closer, Loyola realized that it was in fact two people huddled close together. They were unresponsive to his calls. Drawing closer, Loyola realized he was looking at the faces of his mother, Jean Pomroy, and his aunt, Nellie Pomroy.

"They were close together, and something tells me, although I can't remember for sure, but I seem to think they were holding on to each other's hands, I guess so they wouldn't drift apart," he says.

Both women were silent and still. They might have been dead, but Loyola couldn't be sure, and he knew he had to do what he could to try and save them. For a moment he was seized with anxiety about who he should start with, how he would choose, knowing that even if he could successfully revive one, precious survival time would be lost for the other.

It was no easy task to hold a person in the water and perform life-saving techniques, but it was the only option he had. With mixed emotions, he swam his mother back to the dory and started performing mouth-to-mouth resuscitation, hoping his Aunt Nellie could hang on until he got back to her.

Loyola frantically tried revive his mother. Marjorie has a vivid memory of that moment. She doesn't remember him rescuing her and bringing her back to the dory, but she can remember what she saw later.

"When I regained consciousness, I remember Loyola giving his mom mouth-to-mouth resuscitation. And I remember the *Delroy* captain telling Loyola that it was no use, that she was gone, and that he should look for the children and the others," Marjorie says.

Having already dealt with the excruciating decision of choosing between his forty-four-year-old mother and his fifty-two-year-old aunt—something that tormented him for years afterward—Loyola now faced yet another monumental decision. Should he give up and abandon his mother in order to see if he could revive his aunt and search for his brother Billy, his sisters Sheila and Linda, his brother-in-law, Ernie, and the missing *Delroy* crew members, or should he stay? Driven by the thought that one or more of the others could still be alive, he accepted the harsh reality that he had to leave his mom in hopes of saving another life.

It's almost unimaginable that a twenty-four-year-old man could find the emotional strength to continue swimming around in the cold northwest Atlantic Ocean at midnight, searching for survivors or bodies of loved ones, in what must have been the greatest challenge to anyone's physical endurance.

Loyola Pomroy was determined to expend his last ounce of strength, if necessary, to try and save someone else that night. However, despite his courage, he was tiring and his own survival would soon become an issue. Still, he managed to push himself through the water, all the while straining to see or hear something, a target to swim toward. But it was not to be. There was nothing to hear and nothing to see except the still-burning *Delroy* in the distance.

After weighing the possibilities of finding any more survivors, combined with his worry about those who were clinging to the dory, Loyola made the wise decision to go back to them before he wandered too far away. He could see the flames and smoke coming from *Delroy* on the horizon, but the survivors and the schooner were drifting in different directions and the gap between them was widening, so he couldn't use the schooner as a point of reference for the survivors' location.

"It's kind of strange, I must have had those concerns, but I don't recall feeling tired or having any feelings of panic, from the time I jumped from the schooner or during all of the things that happened in the water. For some reason I seemed to have remained calm through it all," Loyola reflects.

At some point, Leo Bullen and one other crew member alongside the dory decided that they would swim to a nearby island. They could see the shoreline in the moonlight and figured their best chance of survival was to make it to land. They must have reckoned that there would be no shipping in the area to rescue them and that swimming was their only hope. Before leaving, Leo gave Carmel his life jacket because it would be of no benefit to him while swimming. Sadly, the two men didn't make it to the island.

Back at the overturned dory, Carmel, Judy, and Marjorie were managing to hang on by gripping the corners of the life jacket and the strings. Instead of electing one person to wear the life preserver, they spread it across the bottom of the dory so that the three of them could grasp it and help keep them all afloat. Captain Reuben Evans and his son Clarence were still sitting on the bottom of the flat-bottomed boat in relative comfort.

After joining the other five, Loyola knew that they could not survive until daylight, the earliest that anyone would start organizing a search and rescue effort. Even in July, the waters of Placentia Bay were just above freezing, and simply trying to hang on for six or seven hours was not an option. They would certainly succumb to hypothermia long before dawn in the frigid salt water.

Options were few. At one point, Loyola tied the dory's painter around his chest and tried towing the flat-bottomed boat, along with the five other survivors, to the nearest point of land. Loyola was strong, but he soon realized he wasn't superhuman, and though it was a noble and courageous effort, he was forced to accept the fact that there was no option but to hope and pray for a miracle.

Waiting in the water, unable to do anything but cling to the dory, was especially frustrating for Loyola Pomroy. At twenty-four and in good condition, he was accustomed to taking charge of any situation and dealing with it. Accepting that he was no longer able to save any more of his family was not easy, but he was forced to control his emotions and focus on making things as comfortable as possible for those who were still with him, especially his sister Carmel, who was starting to fade.

Marjorie said her cousin was relentless in his determination to see that those remaining would not die. She later wrote, "He was a calming force who tried to bolster their spirits, urging them to remain awake and alert, motivating them to kick their legs to keep up the circulation and stay afloat, trying to tow the dory to the nearest shore, and taking on the responsibility for ensuring they did not slip into the black waters of Placentia Bay, all the while continuing his search efforts for his family."

Whether she had ingested salt water or expended too much energy trying to stay afloat, or if it was because of stress after realizing that her husband, Ernie, and her mom, along with several other family members were missing with little or no hope of survival, Carmel was showing signs of weakening. Whatever the cause, afraid she might let go and slip beneath the waves, Loyola knew he should stay close to his sister.

Meanwhile, as the survivors held on to the dory for dear life, the *Bertha Joyce* was just about to round the tip of the last headland before approaching the entrance to Arnold's Cove. For some reason, at approximately 11:00 p.m., Captain Ray Berkshire opened the top half of the door to the wheelhouse and looked behind the vessel. He doesn't know why he did that, because his primary concern was always what lay directly ahead and not where he had just come from. As fate would have it, six lives hinged on that one quick, backward glance. Captain Berkshire noticed something on the horizon that led him to take a closer look.

"It was a light, but not like a bright searchlight or a ship's light. It was sort of a hazy glow in the distance. It didn't look like fire at first, but I didn't spend any time trying to figure out what it was. I just knew that it wasn't normal and turned our boat around and headed toward whatever it was because it just didn't look right."

At first Captain Berkshire couldn't tell how far away the "glow" was. Judging distance by looking across the ocean at an unknown glow in the dark was impossible. With the engine of the *Bertha Joyce* at full speed, it took twenty minutes before he realized the glow was in fact flames, and it soon became obvious that he was looking at a burning vessel. Because there was no other shipping in the vicinity, Captain Berkshire knew it had to be the *Delroy*. Another twenty to twenty-five minutes would pass before he would be able to confirm his suspicions, because the *Bertha Joyce*'s top speed was about ten knots and he was only halfway to the location of the ill-fated fish collector. He made a mayday distress call on sideband radio to alert the Canadian Coast Guard that a vessel was on fire, but he got no response.

Arriving alongside the burning schooner, Captain Berkshire observed that the wheelhouse was nearly gone and the entire aft section of the *Delroy* badly burnt, but, surprisingly, the front half of the schooner was relatively intact.

"If there was anyone still on board they could have been fairly comfortable up forward at that point," he says.

But Captain Berkshire couldn't see any signs of life on the still-burning vessel, so he asked his crew to stay on deck and scan the waters of Placentia Bay. He noted that the *Delroy*'s dory was not on the deck, so he was hopeful that the crew and passengers were safe.

"Those Grand Bank dories were about twenty feet long and sturdy. We've carried upwards of two tons of salt in those dories, so it would be possible to get fifteen people in one, especially in this case, because some of them were children," he explains.

An experienced captain, Ray Berkshire knew that his search area might be fairly wide because tides and currents could easily push a dead-in-the-water vessel with a cargo of fish on board in one direction and a small dory in another.

But still, he didn't have enough information to pinpoint a probable location of the dory or people, should anyone be in the water, so he decided to meander around the bay, widen his radius from the *Delroy* with each pass, and pray that someone on board his vessel would see or hear something to give them a glimmer of hope.

A mile or so away, just northwest of White Island, Loyola and the others saw the lights of the *Bertha Joyce* as it left the burning schooner. The lights gave them hope that they would be rescued after all. Unfortunately, they had nothing to signal their location, and they were forced to wait and watch as the rescue boat zigzagged across the waters of Placentia Bay.

At one point Captain Berkshire wondered if the crew and passengers had landed on the opposite side of White Island; it was possible they were in that vicinity when they abandoned ship. As he turned the *Bertha Joyce* to check out that possibility, the schooner disappeared from the view of the survivors.

"That was one of the worst low points of the night because we knew we had the chance of being rescued, but now, that one bit of comfort was gone," Loyola says.

Joyfully, a few minutes later, the lights of the *Bertha Joyce* came back into view and, this time, the vessel was heading straight toward them!

"I picked up a small blip on the radar," Captain Berkshire remembers. "I didn't know what it was. It wasn't very big, but I went to check it out because I had nothing else to go on."

A few minutes later, his searchlight spotted Captain Evans and his son on the bottom of the dory, and Loyola, Judy, Carmel, and Marjorie clinging to its sides.

Sometime between midnight and 12:30 a.m., Captain Berkshire manoeuvred the *Bertha Joyce* to the windward side of the survivors, to block the breeze and the lop on the water, while the crew put rubber tires, used as bumpers for docking, over the side.

Captain Ray Berkshire and his son Terry at home in Arnold's Cove

"We put the tires out to give them something to hold onto when we were hauling them on board," he explains.

The crew of the rescue boat got the six survivors down in the forecastle, wrapped them in blankets, and made them as comfortable as possible. Captain Berkshire's brother Dave, who was home on vacation from Halifax, had joined his dad for a trip that day and, fortunately, he knew several life-saving procedures. Seeing that Carmel was nearly dead, Dave immediately started performing CPR and every other technique he knew to try and keep her alive. Thankfully, they worked.

In the wheelhouse, Captain Berkshire set his course for Arnold's Cove. "Loyola was the only one in pretty good condition, and he told me that there was no point looking for the others because they couldn't possibly be alive. It was crucial to get Carmel to hospital, to get the medical attention she desperately needed to keep her from dying, so I headed for Arnold's Cove."

Captain Ray Berkshire (front middle) and Loyola Pomroy (second row) holding awards presented by the Red Cross as "Rescuers Awards" for their heroics in July 1972

All six survivors were taken to Come by Chance hospital and five were released a few hours later. Thanks to the valiant rescue efforts of Dave Berkshire on board the *Bertha Joyce*, Carmel responded positively to treatment and was well enough to go home a few days later.

A search for the missing members of the Pomroy family and three crew members of the *Delroy* was initiated at dawn Friday morning. Jean Pomroy's body was the only one found. It is believed she remained afloat because her lungs had filled with air when Loyola performed artificial respiration on her the previous night.

Searchers also noted that the ill-fated schooner finally slipped beneath the waters of Placentia Bay sometime around 8:00 a.m. Friday.

Memorial Stone for the Pomroy family members lost in July 1972. The stone is located on Merasheen Island. (Photo courtesy of Rita Pomroy)

The loss of Jean Pomroy, age forty-four, her daughters Linda, twelve, Sheila, ten, and son Billy, six, along with her son-in-law, Ernie Pitcher, and her sister-in-law, Nellie Pomroy, fifty-two, in addition to crew members William Garrett, John Yard, and Leo Bullen, was one of the worst marine tragedies in the history of the settlement Placentia Bay, Newfoundland.

However, due to the superb marine capability and intuition of Captain Ray Berkshire—and because of the boundless courage and determination of Loyola Pomroy—Carmel (Pomroy) Pitcher, Marjorie Ennis, Judy Snow, Loyola himself, and *Delroy*'s Captain Reuben Evans and his son Clarence Evans survived.

Certificate of appreciation from the Pomroy family to Captain Ray Berkshire. The certificate hangs on the wall of Captain Berkshire's home.

CHAPTER 2

It's a Family Thing

In February 2012, I met with Claude d'Entremont in Yarmouth, Nova Scotia. We sat in the café at the Mariner's Stadium and talked about his life and philosophies and learned why he was one of the best-known fish processors in the province. Later, the Navigator *magazine published an article based on that interview. About a year after that, I was deeply saddened when Claude passed away after a short illness. The following is what I wrote in the magazine about one of the most respected men in the Nova Scotia fishing industry.*

Claude d'Entremont was manager of a small fish company in southwest Nova Scotia. Inshore Fisheries Ltd. in Lower West Pubnico has been operated successfully by three generations of the d'Entremont family, and the fourth generation is being groomed to take over in a few years.

Claude's grandfather and his grandfather's brother-in-law founded Inshore Fisheries in the 1940s. His dad picked up from Claude's grandfather, and then, a few years after Claude's father passed away in 1977, Claude, his brother, and a couple of cousins took over the business.

One of the cousins, who had also been part-owner of the company for some time, was Jean Guy d'Entremont, perhaps the best-known of the family outside southwest Nova Scotia because he once chaired a high-level national fisheries advisory organization: the now defunct Fisheries Resource Conservation Council (FRCC).

Claude d'Entremont

Meanwhile, like his cousin, Claude was extremely active in serving on industry-related organizations. Some of those include the NS Fish Packers Association, the Science Advisory Committee for George's

Bank, Scotia-Fundy Mobile Gear Committee, Groundfish Allocation Committee, and several groups dealing with US-Canada border issues.

Claude d'Entremont was a highly respected man. Usually referred to as a "true gentleman," Claude was very amiable and easy to talk to. Relaxed and almost always smiling, he talked about his family and the family business with obvious pride.

He would laugh when asked if he ever fished for a living.

"I tried it but I used to get seasick, so I decided to work onshore," he said.

That was a stroke of luck for the company, because managing a groundfish operation for the past thirty years has only benefited from the wisdom and calm approach in decision-making that Claude possessed. Processors of species such as haddock, cod, flounder, perch, and hake have been through tumultuous times during the past three decades in Atlantic Canada and many companies have folded.

Managing your own business is all-consuming, Claude explained.

"You wake up worried about an important decision that you have to make today and you go to bed that night worried about if you made the right decision."

But Claude was not entirely alone when it was time to make big decisions. His younger brother Shawn is president of the company, and though Shawn takes care of the sales and production side of the business, he was always there to listen to his big brother about any issue.

But it doesn't stop there. The other two office staffers, Nancy and Connie, are also family members.

"Generally speaking, we get together and, based on the best information we can get, we hash it out and arrive at a decision. If one of us has a really strong or really bad feeling about going in a certain direction, the rest of us take note and usually don't push it, even with a majority," Shawn said.

Claude used to try to find time to stop thinking about business and concentrate on relaxing. He was a long-time amateur radio operator and, even with today's wireless innovations, he and many of his friends remained true to their hobby. He owned a Goldwing motorcycle that he loved dearly. He also scuba dived and loved hunting. Claude tried golfing once but decided it wasn't for him.

"I discovered that golfing was just a way to ruin an otherwise perfectly nice walk," he joked.

Chatting about his ham radio hobby versus modern wireless phones, Claude told us an amusing anecdote about the new technology.

"I remember once when I was deer hunting. I was sitting there quietly in a tree stand with my gun ready as soon as I saw a deer—suddenly, my phone rang. I looked at the name and number and saw that it was a fellow I was trying to make a deal with, so I answered. I made the deal to sell one of our boats to him right there," he laughed, citing both an upside and a downside of cellphones. He might have lost the opportunity to get a deer, but, on the other hand, he wrapped up a successful business transaction.

Family-operated businesses are common among Nova Scotia Acadians. In fact, the principles of "family" seem to be an important cornerstone in the Acadian French culture in southwest Nova Scotia. The entire community seems to look after its own.

Claude d'Entremont was the eldest of eight children. His sister Carmelle is the youngest and, although she is not part of the company, her name has certainly been prominent. Several of the company's vessels have been named after her, beginning with *Carmelle #1* through to

Carmelle #6. The company currently owns and operates three vessels, including the *Carmelle #3* and *Carmelle #6.*

Their other vessel, *Poseidon Princess,* has proven to be what Claude describes as an "adventure." He chuckled when asked what that meant and passed it off as a long story, "too long for this conversation." All three vessels are in excess of sixty feet in length.

After forty-plus years involved in the most dangerous industry in the country, Claude said he and his family had been blessed with good luck.

"In all those years, only once did I have to call a vessel in from sea because of an emergency," he said. That incident involved the tragic on-shore death of a family member who was related to the captain on one of the company's vessels.

"I called the captain and said, 'You have to come in—I can't tell you why right now but you must come in.' The captain said, 'Okay, but can I ask who (on the boat) does it directly involve?'"

"I had to tell him that it was him . . . that was hard."

Claude was very much a family man. He was married, a father of a son and daughter, and a grandfather to three. He always smiled broadly as he talked about his mother, who was unable to care for herself at the end and decided to enter a seniors' home. Claude said one evening he thanked his mom for everything she had done for him and his seven siblings.

"Mom said that she didn't do much, but I told her she was wrong about that—she was always there for the family, constantly. When we all came home from school, when we came home from being away or whatever, she was always there, and that was all that mattered to us. Not everyone is so lucky, especially many children today," he said.

Claude talked philosophically about many issues in the fishing industry, ranging from the return of haddock on George's Bank, to the damage to groundfish stocks by burgeoning herds of grey seals, to the foolhardiness of many people these days.

It frustrated him to see how people didn't think twice about paying hundreds of dollars to attend a sports or music event every month or spending thousands of dollars on high-tech toys—but if the cost of milk went up two cents a litre, they got upset and angry and refused to buy it and demanded reductions, even if it meant putting a farmer out of business.

"There's something very wrong with that way of thinking," he would say.

But, positive thinker that he was, Claude soon moved the conversation to a less frustrating topic. For him, the bottle was always half full.

CHAPTER 3

Like a Duck on the Water

Andrew "Chum" Greenham was one of Twillingate's many famous schooner captains in the early to mid-1900s. The son of Captain Isaac Greenham, Andrew was nicknamed "Chummy" when he was a young boy, and even as he grew older the moniker stuck but was shortened to "Chum." Even some of his friends had never heard his real name in all his ninety-three years.

Andrew was still called "Chummy" when he first went to the Labrador fishery in 1907 as a shareman on board a fishing schooner. He was fourteen and he begged his father to take him as part of the crew on the family schooner *Fleet Queen*, but Captain Isaac refused, explaining that the young lad should stay home and help his mom with all the chores of summer.

The *Fleet Queen* sailed out of Twillingate one day in early June, leaving behind a very discouraged lad. But young Chummy was determined, and when he heard that Captain Loder from nearby Back Harbour was still looking for a shareman for the summer's voyage, Chum walked, mostly ran, across to the north side of Twillingate Island to try and convince the skipper to take him on. Captain Loder was hesitant, but when Chum stretched the truth a bit, saying that he had both his father and mother's blessing, Captain Loder finally agreed.

"Okay then, my boy, get a bit of clothes, and a pair of rubber boots, and be here tomorrow morning before five o'clock because we sail by six," said the captain.

Captain Chum Greenham shows off a nice Atlantic salmon.

Young Chum was at the Back Harbour wharf long before daylight the next morning, waiting for the skipper and other crew members to set sail for Labrador.

Chum Greenham worked as hard or harder than the veteran fishermen that summer and proved himself a very worthy shareman. In fact, on the way home to Twillingate in the fall, Skipper Loder called the crew together to talk about young Chummy's "share." Because Chum was just fourteen and on his first trip, the captain asked the crew if Chum should be paid only a half share.

"Oh no, sir," the crew all responded vigorously. "Chum gets a full share like us, or we only get the same as he does," said the crew spokesman.

"If the rights of it was known, he should get more than the rest of us," said one fellow.

Andrew "Chum" Greenham had earned his stripes as a full-time schooner fisherman at the tender age of fourteen.

The following year, 1908, Chum fished with his father, but if Captain Isaac was thinking that his son would be his successor as skipper of the *Fleet Queen*, he soon had to think again. Chum was much too impatient for the wait. Only one year later, when Chum was just sixteen, he heard that William Ashbourne's company was looking for a captain for one of its schooners. Undeterred by his young age, Chum went to see Ashbourne.

"I'm here because I heard you were looking for a skipper for one of your schooners," Chum said.

"Yes, Chum, that's right. Do you know someone who is interested?" Mr. Ashbourne asked.

"I am, sir," Chum said.

The businessman was surprised at the teenage boy's boldness to ask for such a responsible position, but he had heard about Chum's ability as a crewman, so he paused to think about the proposal.

Recognizing that Mr. Ashbourne was actually considering his offer,

Chum jumped in with what might be considered a negotiating point, albeit a risky one.

"If you give me the chance, sir, I'll hire a crew of young fellas my age and younger. That way, there will be no dispute about who is skipper."

William Ashbourne had become a very successful businessman through taking calculated risks, but he also knew that giving control of a vessel to a teenager whose intent was to hire more teenagers would probably be one of his riskiest decisions of all. But he took the chance and shook hands with Chum to seal the deal.

Twillingate harbour circa 1920s

Chum Greenham didn't disappoint William Ashbourne. With his crew of "rough and ready" teenagers, the youthful skipper caught so many fish that they made a rare two trips to Labrador that summer.

By 1926, Chum Greenham was a very experienced and highly respected schooner captain. William Ashbourne had been keeping a steady eye on Chum's accomplishments, and one day while he was planning for the summer schooner fishery, he called the young skipper to his office.

"Chum, I've been very pleased with your work, and so I have an offer for you to consider," he said. "We've added a new and bigger schooner called the *Stanley Smith* to our fleet and I'm wondering if you'd like to take her over."

Before Chum could answer, Mr. Ashbourne continued with a little additional information that he wanted Chum to know.

"They say she's an unlucky schooner, Chum," Mr. Ashbourne explained. "She has never caught a full load of fish."

Chum Greenham had beaten a lot of odds in his life, and although he admitted to being a bit "uneasy" about taking on a supposed unlucky ship, he didn't hesitate.

"I will gladly take the *Stanley Smith*, sir, and even though I can't guarantee you I'll get a full load of fish, I will give it a good shot," he told Ashbourne.

The next day, Chum contacted his regular crew, and because the *Stanley Smith* was a large schooner, he hired two additional crew members. In a few hours, all the young men were fitting out their vessel in hopes of a great summer on the Labrador Coast.

After taking their new schooner out for a couple of test runs, it soon became obvious that the *Stanley Smith* was a great sailing vessel.

"She's the best sailing schooner in the Ashbourne fleet—she's real fast, and the harder the wind blows the better she likes it—she's like a duck on the water in any wind," Chum told his friends.

Skipper Chum and his band of young, bold sharemen on board the *Stanley Smith* set out in June for Cutthroat Islands on Labrador's south coast, where the crew was eager to set cod traps. Whether it was in keeping with the schooner's reputation as a bad-luck schooner or pure coincidence, the 1926 fishery would be one that Captain Chum Greenham would remember till the day he died at the age of ninety-three.

Upon arrival in Labrador, Captain Chum and his crew quickly set out the cod gear, excited about their new schooner and in high hopes for a good summer season. A full load of codfish would be extra nice that year because their relatively new schooner had never landed a bumper catch and was considered an unlucky boat. Low landings in the first couple of weeks worried some of the crew, who wondered if it was an omen of a poor voyage. Maybe the *Stanley Smith* really was a bad-luck schooner after all, they thought. Even Captain Chum admitted that the thought crossed his mind, too.

Weekly landings didn't improve much over the summer months, but Captain Greenham was determined to go home with a full load, so he continued fishing on the Labrador Coast much later than usual and fished hard every day. By October 24, the *Stanley Smith*'s fish holds were filled to the hatches with about 3,000 quintals of salt cod.

In preparation for the journey back home to Twillingate, the crew was instructed to stow fishing gear below deck, clean out the pumps, and fasten down the trap skiffs and the punt, along with barrels of cod livers and other product on deck. Buoyed by anticipation of a good voyage, some of the crew members laughed that they had proved the *Stanley Smith* to be a lucky vessel after all.

But the trip home was just beginning.

There was a beautiful sunrise in southern Labrador on Monday, October 25, 1926. A pleasant north-northwest breeze was a fair wind for sailing south—the perfect day for the crew of a fine sailing schooner to head home. The *Stanley* was low in the water, laden with the full load of fish, but still they made excellent time all day. Late at night they were ready to cross the Strait of Belle Isle to the island of Newfoundland.

Captain Chum looked at his weather glass. The barometer, or "glass," was the only forecasting instrument on board schooners in those days and was usually a reliable indicator of impending bad weather. The glass didn't suggest anything to be concerned about, so Captain Chum decided that, with fair winds and clear skies, he would sail all night instead of anchoring in a nearby harbour on the Labrador side of the Straits to wait for daylight. He instructed four-hour watches, with himself and three crewmen taking the first watch that night. Two men were on the bow and two on the quarterdeck. Each would share one-hour stints on the wheel, located toward the stern of the vessel—there was no wheelhouse on the *Stanley Smith*.

The crewmen were in high spirits as the fine sailing schooner plowed white water.

"Won't be long now before we give our women a nice kiss," sang out one crewman.

But the kisses would have to wait.

Although the weather glass was still indicating good barometric pressure, the midnight sky had darkened and winds had strengthened enough that *Stanley*'s leeward rails were dragging through the water and its decks were awash in increasingly heavy seas. Ordering the crew to lower the mainsail and to double-reef the others, Captain Chum set their course due south and lashed himself to the wheel—just in case.

Temperatures dropped and, by daylight on Tuesday, powerful winds whipped snow across the faces of the worried crewmen.

By mid-morning, winds were raging at gale-force strength as Captain Greenham ordered the men to lower the jib and most other sails to avoid capsizing. The crew also shuttered the entrance to the forecastle and kept the pumps going almost constantly because heavy seas were now constantly washing across the schooner's decks. Despite solid lashings, the barrels on deck broke loose and smashed against the bulwarks. The deck of the *Stanley Smith* had become an incredibly dangerous environment as pieces of wood and metal were tossed around in sea water. All the men tied themselves to whatever seemed secure and worked feverishly for hours to stay out of harm's way. Skipper Chum yelled to the men to keep debris away from the bulwarks to allow the waters to wash from the decks.

"If necessary, chop the rails as well and let it all go overboard, because if you don't we will sink!" he shouted.

By dark that evening, there was hardly anything left on deck. Even the punt, which was lashed down bottom-up, had been seriously damaged. Without sails the *Stanley Smith* was running with the winds and seas, although the skipper tried to maintain a southerly course by working the rudder very hard. One young fellow was so certain that they would all die that night that he wanted to get it over with. He tried to untie his rope and allow himself to wash overboard. Fortunately, the other crewmen were able to subdue him. Captain Greenham wondered out loud how much longer they could last.

Amazingly, the *Stanley Smith* was still floating as winds abated on Wednesday, October 27, but the captain and crew were battered, hungry, and tired. No one had eaten in more than twenty-four hours. Someone had taken a look down in the galley and reported back with the bad news that all their food had been tossed around in the storm and water leaking down from the deck had ruined everything. Adding to their misery, the barrels of fresh water that were on deck had also been washed overboard.

Ordering sails to be raised again, Captain Chum tried to figure out where they were and set course for what he hoped would be the tip of Newfoundland's Northern Peninsula. His reckoning was true, and about midnight the *Stanley Smith* dropped anchor in Quirpon harbour.

Captain Chum Greenham (standing on rock) sings the Johnny Poker as men launch a house in Twillingate.

Although it was the dead of night in the sleepy little Newfoundland community, Skipper Chum knew that his men couldn't wait until morning to have food and water. Lowering the battered punt over the side, he and his "second hand" and brother-in-law, Stanley Elliot, managed to keep the punt afloat and rowed to the community wharf. From there they walked to the home of the local merchant, whom Chum had met before.

When the merchant opened the door, he couldn't believe his eyes.

"Where in the world did you come from tonight, Chum?" he asked.

After listening to Captain Greenham's story, the merchant took the men to his store and offered them food, dry clothes, and anything else they needed.

In later years, Captain Chum often talked about the Quirpon merchant's kindness that night. The young captain said the merchant even gave the crew his motorboat to take with them in case they needed it to go ashore or use as a lifeboat if anything else went wrong. While the crew made repairs to the schooner for the trip home, they discovered that the weather glass was not working properly. That explained the false readings on the day they left Labrador.

Captain Greenham and his crew made it home to Twillingate at the end of October, tired and weary after the battle to survive a vicious storm, but very thankful and feeling lucky that their first voyage on the so-called unlucky *Stanley Smith* in 1926 had not been their final voyage.

CHAPTER 4

The Fish Ladies

On my travels through Atlantic Canada, I have been blessed to meet hundreds of wonderful men and women. Among the most fascinating women I met along the way, two of them have a lot in common. They are close to the same age, they have very similar personalities, share many of the same interests, and they even look a lot alike. And they are both known as "Fish Ladies." One lives in New Brunswick and the other in Newfoundland. It is my great pleasure to introduce to you two of the nicest and hardest-working people in Atlantic Canada, Marilyn and Karen.

THE FISH LADY OF LEWISPORTE, NEWFOUNDLAND: MARILYN KINDEN

If you worked sixteen hours a day, seven days a week for most of the year, you would know a little bit about what it's like to be Marilyn Kinden.

Known to many as the "Fish Lady," Marilyn and her husband, Everett, run a busy retail fish business called Treats from the Sea. Based near Lewisporte on Newfoundland's northeast coast, the family business started in the mid-1980s when Everett bought lobsters from a local fisherman and sold them from the back of his pickup truck.

The idea was to pick up a few dollars pocket money. Today, the couple has grown the business to go beyond fish, and they have included several other family members along with several non-family employees.

Driving east from Lewisporte on the Road to the Isles toward Twillingate, you can't miss their lobster pound and retail outlet. A huge twenty-six-foot lobster sitting on the north side of the highway just in front of the store is more than enough to catch your attention.

The 12,000-pound-capacity holding tanks inside the building are also likely to garner a second glance, not to mention the bright red fish and chips van situated a hundred feet to the left of the store.

Marilyn Kinden shows off a lobster in her store.

Government regulations no longer allow the Kindens to purchase lobsters directly from fishermen, but they only buy locally caught lobsters and purchase far more than one pickup load at a time these days.

While lobster is still one of their main products, Marilyn and Everett have expanded the business to include fresh crab, cod (salted as well as fresh), mackerel, salmon, caplin, kippers, seal flippers (in season), shrimp, and many other species—including mussels supplied by Terry Mills, owner of Norlantic Mussels Farms in nearby Botwood.

Marilyn realized that the Road to the Isles had a limited customer base, so she decided to go mobile with Treats from the Sea. Four days a week she fills a large cube van with fish and drives to Gander, Grand Falls, and Botwood, where she sells directly from the truck. She operates the van from April until just after Labour Day and comes back again for a couple of weeks in December, when people like to stock up on fish supplies for the winter.

Treats from the Sea

Marilyn Kinden is a high-energy and outgoing person who thrives on interacting with people. In other words, she's perfect for her job.

Her customers cross the demographic spectrum, and that's the way she likes it. One minute she's chatting with a young mom and the next minute she's joking with a retired judge. They're all the same to Marilyn.

Several years ago, she had a customer who was very difficult to deal with. He was demanding beyond reason and at times was downright rude. Trying her best to honour the age-old maxim that the customer was always right, Marilyn bit her tongue and said nothing. But Marilyn Kinden can't be silent for too long, and something had to give.

One day, the customer was being particularly difficult.

"He was buying a salmon, and every one I took out of the box was too big, too small, not the right colour, it was too slimy or too something—there was no way of pleasing him, and he was also rude," she explains.

That was the moment Marilyn decided that maintaining her sanity was more important than losing a customer, and Mr. Rude and Impossible got an earful that he never forgot. Interestingly, he continued to be a customer for years later—without a single murmur of discontent.

In 2011, Everett and Marilyn brought their daughter, Chelsea, into their business and set up a fish and chips van next to the lobster pound. Chelsea's Fish and Chips is just part of the Kindens' many expansion plans for their Road to the Isles business.

Among other things, Marilyn talks excitedly about building a docking facility nearby to accommodate the busy boat traffic in Notre Dame Bay. Lewisporte is home to a large fleet of both powerboats and sailboats. Several inshore fishing vessels also frequent the area.

Five years ago, Marilyn decided to start fundraising for charity. Many of her customers said they liked to cook lobster in salt water and asked if they could have some from the pound to take home with them. Of course she obliged, but she had an idea. Marilyn realized that people don't expect something for nothing, so she gave people an option of making a contribution to a charity in return for a bag of salt water. She placed a donation container in the area where people could voluntarily drop a loonie or toonie, and at the end of the season Marilyn donates the contributions to her charity of choice. This past year she raised $2,060 for the Children's Wish Foundation (Lewisporte Chapter). Other charities she has helped include the Shriners, SPCA, Janeway Children's Hospital, and Daffodil Place.

Giant lobster model outside the Treats from the Sea store

Marilyn says they've managed to keep their fish prices at nearly the same level for the past eight years. Inflationary costs have been absorbed through increased volume. She also boasts prices lower than supermarkets for fish. In some cases, she says, her prices are substantially lower.

Marilyn has advertised, but the popularity of the business has largely been through word of mouth. She loves to tell the story about a cab driver from New York who visited for a week and had supper every evening at their facility. Marilyn says the cabbie was chatting with a customer in New York one day when the customer mentioned that he had recently returned from Newfoundland. The driver was intrigued because, coincidentally, he and his wife had booked a vacation to Newfoundland for the summer of 2012, so he had a lot of questions.

"Well, the guy told the cab driver that if he went to Central (Newfoundland) he must look up this fish shop. Sure enough, the cabbie did look us up, and every evening for a week he and his wife stopped by for supper before going back to their hotel in Lewisporte," Marilyn laughs.

When the fishing season ends, Marilyn and Everett, along with their son Chad, turn their attention to a whole different business—one that started even smaller than the fish business.

Years ago, when Everett would cut a Christmas tree for their home, he'd get another two or three for a neighbour or family member or an elderly family. The requests from other friends and neighbours increased, so one day Everett thought that cutting Christmas trees for sale might be another way to pick up a few dollars.

Marilyn says while most people think that growing a tree and selling it for $40 is easy money, reality is a different matter.

"For starters, it takes about nine years to grow a tree, and when you factor in fertilizer costs, herbicides, vehicle and fuel costs and salaries, there is not a very wide margin of profit."

They've leased fifty acres of Crown land but so far have not developed all of it.

And still there is more. Everett also owns an outfitting business near Millertown in Central Newfoundland.

Kinden's Quinn Lake Outfitters has a drive-in hunting and fishing camp that includes a Red Seal Chef.

Marilyn has a role in that business as well but, to most Newfoundlanders, Marilyn Kinden remains "The Fish Lady of Lewisporte."

THE LOBSTER LADY OF LORNEVILLE, NEW BRUNSWICK: KAREN McCAVOUR

People say nice things about Karen McCavour from Lorneville, New Brunswick.

Karen McCavour working the lobster boilers

Many say she has a kind heart. And she does, but years ago, when Karen was just five years old, her heart was generous but it was not healthy. She's fine now, but she needed surgery to correct the problem. Years later, when her son Bronson was born, Karen was devastated when doctors told her that he also had a heart defect. However, it was not related to the heart problem she had as a child. Happily, too, Bronson, like his mom, is doing just fine and he's a very active and normal sixteen-year-old.

Now in her forties, Karen is giving back to the hospital that conducted her and Bronson's surgeries, and she's doing so in a big way. I'll tell you more about that on another page, but for now let me introduce you to her.

Karen Vickers McCavour has always been the outdoorsy, hands-on type.

In her high school days, Karen decided to take advantage of the industrial programs that were available through the school system and took a welding course. She became the first female in New Brunswick to earn two welding certificates. She's also an avid big-game hunter and knows her way around a fishing boat, too.

But these days Karen leaves the boat work to her husband, Captain Kenny McCavour, and she takes care of a new and flourishing fish business located on their home property in Lorneville, on the outskirts of Saint John.

A few years ago, the price of lobster dropped dramatically and, like all his peers, Kenny was finding it tough to make a decent living. Karen was a stay-at-home mom, so she decided to try and make a few dollars on the side and started cooking lobster to sell from her home. In the beginning, her customers were scarcely more than a few neighbours and friends, but, through word of mouth, demand grew quickly to include strangers. It wasn't long before Karen knew she was on to something good.

Kenny and Karen's love of hunting led to naming Kenny's fishing vessel *Whitetail*, and Karen decided to extend the same name to her company, Whitetail Fisheries.

As her business continued to expand, Karen knew that she needed to contact local authorities about issues like licensing and whatever else she might need to know about operating a business. "I called and asked what I needed. I asked for an inspector to come by. He did, and the first thing he said was that I needed a separate building. So we went to work and built a store ourselves, mostly ourselves, and soon we had a building ready to go."

Karen does some advertising, but word had spread that there was a "fish lady" running a cooked lobster business in Lorneville and she became an extremely busy woman. Karen laughs when she explains that she started cooking lobster with a single spaghetti pot and then moved up to a restaurant-size one, and eventually purchased a large 150-pound pot. "That's my baby now," she laughs.

"It wasn't long before we had to build an addition on the store to give customers who were waiting to be served a proper place to stand in a shelter," she says.

Karen the outdoorswoman and hunter

One thing led to another, and soon several local crafts people approached Karen to see if she would sell their goods on a commission basis. It was about then the idea of donating to the Halifax children's hospital came along.

While the business has grown leaps and bounds in the past few years, the bulk of Karen's work is still primarily about what she started out doing: selling cooked or live lobster during the lobster fishing season in southern New Brunswick, about three months in spring and then again in fall through to late January or early February.

Karen and Sue Roach, ready to cook

Karen has a lobster holding pound on her home property that is supplied with ocean water through a pumping system from the sea nearby. Near the pound is where you will find her store, which has lobster tanks, cooking facilities, crafts, and more. Karen also sells clams and other fish products, but her "biggy" is still lobster, she says.

Kenny and his crew catch the lobster and land it at their wharf. Karen meets the boat on her tractor and brings the live lobster from the wharf to the pound.

Along with her full-time employee, Susan "Sue" Roach, Karen runs a very busy operation seven days a week. The busiest time is during the fall lobster fishery, which peaks leading up to Christmas. At this time, it gets so busy that every minute needs to be planned and organized. With Kenny and his crew working nearly around the clock on the boat, Karen sometimes has to enlist her two sons, Eric and Bronson, to help out while she and Sue race the clock at the store and the pound from seven o'clock in the morning until midnight. In those weeks, there is barely time to catch a nap or a meal. In fact, Karen says that some of their regular customers realize how busy they are and bring them snacks or even full lunches. "That is very nice and very touching," Karen says.

Sue has become such an integral part of the business that Karen says she has to share her title. She now describes herself as just one of the two "Lobster Ladies" of Lorneville.

Ironically, both "lobster ladies" have developed allergies to lobster—but only if they eat it. Lucky for them, too, because some people with allergies can't even be in the same room where lobster and other shellfish are cooked. Karen says the food allergy may not be a bad thing because it keeps them from sampling the goods too much.

Karen decided that she would give back some of her profit and she knew exactly what her charity of choice was. The IWK children's hospital in Halifax often fundraises for new equipment and other things, and since that hospital was largely responsible for restoring her and her son's health, it was a perfect match.

Some of the commissions from craft sales go into the IWK pot, along with money raised through several other schemes including a huge lobster cook-up party she and Kenny hold once a year at their cottage. Last year, 300 people showed up for that event and left thousands of dollars for the IWK fund, accounting for a sizable portion of the $18,200 they contributed to IWK in 2013.

In the off-season, when there is time to relax, Karen likes to travel. She and Kenny enjoy hiking and sometimes travel to Western Canada to hike in the mountains. They also enjoy hiking in Cape Breton. When they want to go somewhere warm, Karen says Barbados is a favourite southern destination. They hunt big game as often as possible; in fact, they enjoy hunting in Central Newfoundland. The McCavours collect moose and deer antlers and sometimes make chandeliers out of them. You can see some samples in their lodge.

CHAPTER 5

Salt of the Earth

It's hard to write about Vernon Petten when you're only allowed a couple of pages. That's barely enough for an intro to a man who has spent more than sixty years fishing and who has been a volunteer extraordinaire at home and abroad.

Still living in Port de Grave, Newfoundland, the town where he was born eighty years ago, Vernon fished every species native to local waters. After chatting with him for an hour or so, you will undoubtedly hear about his passion for tuna fishing. Whether it was the size and majesty of the large bluefin or the big financial prize it paid back in Vernon's heyday, there was something about fishing tuna that seemed to get his adrenaline going like none other.

He likes to talk about his most successful tuna year and one particular trip. It was just before his youngest son, Blair's, wedding. The weather was bad and he could only get two deckhands to go with him, but his senses were telling him that there were tuna out there and, as far as he was concerned, they had his name on them. Blair was concerned that his dad wouldn't be back in time for the wedding, but Vernon assured him that he would be home and with a good voyage under his belt. He was right, but it was only through a bit of good luck that he didn't come back seriously injured.

While fishing in rough seas, Vernon was knocked off balance and went sliding across the deck, stopping only when his head smacked into a piece of steel equipment. The crew members wanted to get the skipper to the hospital, but Vernon was having none of that—there was work to be done, and a two- or three-inch gash in his head was no excuse to go home.

Captain Vernon Petten mending trawl with son Blair in Port de Grave

"No, no, we're not going anywhere—you fellas can patch me up and we're gonna go back fishing," he stated firmly. The men did as the captain commanded, and despite a wide cut in his head that was bleeding profusely, they managed to bandage the wound sufficiently to stop the bleeding.

"The doctor told me later that they did a good job, although the dent is still there now," he says, pointing to his head.

"And that turned out to be a real good trip. We got eight tuna and I think we made $60,000 after expenses because they were big ones." Vernon smiles, adding that he didn't have any problems getting crew for his next tuna trip that year.

He relishes talking about his early days fishing with his father, Henry Petten. The Newfoundland fishery consisted of mainly salt cod back then with very little return on their investment, but he says they worked hard and always managed to get by, even when they were paid a measly two cents a pound.

When his dad wanted to get a new and bigger boat, there was plenty of discussion about affordability. That's when Vernon proposed that he and his dad build the boat themselves—from the keel to the wheelhouse. Vernon was young and his dad was a little hesitant, but he decided that it was the only way they could afford a new vessel, so he agreed to give it a try. They cut their own logs, hauled them out from the woods, and went to work on building a longliner. While it might not have been a fancy construction, they built a good sea boat that served the family well. That was when Vernon got the boatbuilding bug. He perfected his construction skills through hard work, and today he holds the status of Master Boat Builder. He has built eleven longliners and repaired many more.

His church has always played a large role in Vernon's life. He's been a board member and treasurer of the Pentecostal Church in Port de Grave for more than fifty years. He has also served on the board of the Gideon's Society for years. Through his church, he also travelled to different parts of the world, spending his own money to provide labour, particularly his carpentry skills, to rebuilding churches and other buildings in regions that had been devastated by hurricanes or other disasters. He went to Montserrat in the West Indies in 1990, St. Lucia in the Caribbean and Zambia, Africa, in 1991, and back to Africa again in 1997.

Vernon is not the type to boast about his travels. Instead, he enjoys talking about his interest in the various cultures he observed there and shares stories about his adventures when trying to construct something from sparse building materials.

He also volunteers at home—a lot. He's been a member of the Coast Guard Auxiliary for years. He also volunteered with the Heritage Society, the local museum, the Port de Grave Harbour Authority, and the list goes on.

Vernon is a shining example of what volunteerism stands for. He does things for the sheer satisfaction and joy of being able to help those less fortunate.

One of the pastors at his church tells a story about Vernon that sums him up very well.

Pastor K. M. Bess said, "There was a family in our community in need of a house because the house they occupied was inadequate for the coming winter. It was then that Vernon volunteered his entire fall, day and night, putting his carpentry skills to work, and with little help from anyone else he built this family a house, from its foundation to the kitchen cabinets. I personally witnessed him volunteering his time every day, including Christmas Eve, putting the finishing touches on the house to get the family in for Christmas Day. The work was completed and the house stands today as a representation of selfless giving, thanks to Vernon Petten."

People noticed Vernon's goodness and nominated him for several prestigious awards, most of which he was granted. He received the

Newfoundland and Labrador Volunteer Medal in 2001 and the Queen's Golden Jubilee Medal in 2002. He was also awarded the Queen's Diamond Jubilee Medal in 2012 and was inducted into the Navigator Mariner's Hall of Fame in 2008.

Vernon and his wife, Shirley, live in a modest but cozy home which he built himself when they were married sixty years ago in Port de Grave. He told me that on a couple of occasions Shirley hinted that it might be nice to have a new, more modern home—especially for occasions when they have family visiting. But Vernon is a humble man who sees nothing wrong with their old traditional house in

Shirley and Vernon Petten

which they raised six children and had a good life. There is no doubt that they could afford a much larger and more expensive property, but fancy houses don't impress Vernon Petten.

At eighty years of age, Vernon doesn't go to sea very often these days. Blair has taken over most of the family business, but Vernon is still very active in the decision-making process and still plays a very hands-on role in the enterprise.

While tuna fishing might have been his most interesting fishery to prosecute, Vernon says his favourite meal of fish is cod and smiles as he pays Shirley a nice compliment.

"They say you've never tasted good fish until you've had Shirley Petten's pan-fried cod," he says, nodding his agreement as Shirley laughs.

Lucky for me, I had just sat down at the kitchen table in their home to a huge plateful of Shirley's wonderful pan-fried cod, complete with potatoes, scruncheons, and all the fixin's.

Just the aroma from the hot, heaping dinner plate was enough for me to know that I didn't need Vernon's convincing about Shirley's cooking skills.

CHAPTER 6

Tabusintac's Troubled Year

The town of Tabusintac in northeastern New Brunswick, along with several neighbouring communities, is still reeling after the tragic lobster season of 2013. Three fishermen died in the early morning hours of May 18 when their fishing vessel struck a sandbar and capsized. The tragedy came on the heels of another blow to the fishing community less than two weeks prior. On May 5, fire totally destroyed five fishing vessels that were docked at the wharf in Tabusintac. Several other vessels were damaged, and more were moved away from the wharf just in time to escape the same fate.

And then, on May 27, just nine days after the full reality of the most tragic incident to hit that area in decades was starting to sink in, four more vessels grounded on a sandbar, but this time luck was on the side of the crews. The tide was low, the wind and seas were calm, and everyone survived without serious incident. Later in the day, the boats were able to move off the sandbar under their own steam at high tide.

Losing a fishing boat means losing the primary tool of a fisherman's trade. Without a vessel, he or she can't work, and that leaves them without a means to financially survive and support their families.

As devastating as the loss of five vessels to fire was to the small fishing village of Tabusintac, the loss of three lives was a terrible blow. Replacing vessels would obviously mean a huge financial burden and create severe difficulty for those affected, but it pales in comparison to the loss of three productive and relatively young men. Vessels can be replaced, but lives cannot.

The year 2013 was one that lobster fishermen and their families in Tabusintac and area wish they could forget—but they know they never will.

Anxiety started early in the lobster season for fishermen in northeastern New Brunswick fishing communities. Prices for the delicious crustacean plummeted before the spring season officially opened and, like many of their counterparts in all of Atlantic Canada, fishermen in Tabusintac debated whether it was worth their time to set traps. Some left their boats at the wharf for a few days rather than fish for such a measly return on their investment. Fuel, vessel insurance, crew salaries, and every other expense connected to their fishing enterprise continued to increase, and prices at or below $3 per pound were barely enough to pay the bills, let alone make a small profit.

But finally, push came to shove and buyers increased the price, and eventually fishermen decided that they would untie their boats, thinking that if they could catch a lot of lobsters in a short period, they just might be lucky enough to make ends meet.

Trap setting day (season opening) was April 29 and fishermen couldn't ask for better weather, so most boats that were docked at McEachern's Point wharf in Tabusintac were boarded before daylight. More than thirty vessels were steaming out the harbour at dawn.

Weather turned bad after opening day and some boats got out only a couple times that week, so it was a relief when the weather forecast called for calm seas and sunny skies on Monday, May 6. But the good forecast was muted for many in the early morning hours of Sunday, May 5.

Robbie Wishart, a young fisherman in Tabusintac, was abruptly awakened by the sound of his phone ringing just before 3:00 a.m. on Sunday morning. It was his cousin Gordie Wishart saying there was a fire at the wharf and it looked like there may be more than one boat burning. Robbie jumped out of bed, woke his dad, and ran to his truck. A few minutes later, he arrived at McEachern's wharf. Gordie was already there and making calls on his cellphone to alert as many boat owners as he could. Shortly, the father-son fishing team of Billy and Jamie McEachern, who lived near the dock, also arrived. Word spread fast through Tabusintac that morning, and soon several fishermen, including Peter McEachern, Robbie's dad, John, Weldon Harding, and others were on the scene as well.

Robbie says he could hardly believe what he was seeing. Amazingly, five vessels were all burning intensely. The men knew it was impossible to attempt to move the burning boats, so the only thing they could do was to try and move other vessels still untouched by the flames out of harm's way. But moving forty- to forty-five-foot lobster boats, most of them carrying approximately 500 gallons of fuel, is easier said than done, especially in a small harbour. Tabusintac wharf was designed to accommodate hardly more than twenty boats, but on May 5, 2013, there were twice that many docked, meaning several vessels were docked side by side, as many as three or four deep.

Five vessels burning at Tabusintac wharf (Photo courtesy of Gail Harding)

That was Robbie Wishart's dilemma. His own boat, *Ocean Spray*, was docked just ahead of the burning vessels, but his was on the inside at the wharf and he had to move those outside first before saving his own vessel.

Moving a forty-five-foot lobster boat can't be done in a matter of a few seconds, like you can with small rowboats. The engines have to be started and the boats manoeuvred around, one at a time, or they have to be towed. And that's what Robbie and the others did to get away from the intense heat and flames. They could start the engines on some boats, but others were locked, so Robbie and the other rescuers hitched a line to their boats and towed those away.

Working feverishly, the men moved approximately fifteen vessels away from the flames and across the harbour to safety, but while they did a great job, there was no way to save all the boats from danger. Some vessels were totally destroyed and sunk, while a few others were scorched but were not a total loss.

Fishermen in Tabusintac have a collective uneasy feeling about what caused the fires on board five of their fishing boats that night.

It was a calm night and boats were not pushing against each other by wave action. There was a watchman at the wharf, but he went home as usual, about midnight, at the end of his regular shift, just a few hours before fishermen and boat owners would start arriving at the wharf. It might be pure coincidence, but the boats that burned were the only five that had backed into the wharf rather than rafted side by side, parallel to the dock like the rest. But the strangest thing that everyone, including the police, couldn't seem to understand is that all five vessels seemed to be burning at the same intensity and at the same rate—all at the same time. Two of the five were fibreglass construction and three were wooden hulls. While the fibreglass burned more quickly and intensely than the wooden boats, it seemed to Robbie and the other fishermen who were at the wharf that all five were burning equally at first, indicating the fires started on all boats at the same time. Police are still investigating, but so far they have not found enough evidence to charge anyone with any wrongdoing.

The fire was a devastating blow to the owners of the vessels. Although some insurance was carried, it wasn't nearly enough to cover their losses. However, they were determined to carry on. Within forty-eight hours, the boat owners had rented or borrowed vessels from fishermen in their hometown or in neighbouring communities and were back on the water trying to salvage something from the troubled lobster fishery of 2013.

All five were back on the water a couple of days later, among them veteran Captain Weldon Harding and a very close friend of his, Captain Ian Benoit. Ian had fished as a crew member with Weldon for eight years. In fact, Weldon and his wife, Genevieve, both say Ian was like a son to them.

A big concern for area fishermen in May was the ever-shifting sandbars located about four kilometres off the coastline from McEachern's Point wharf where fishermen docked their vessels. The sediment on the sandy bottom is constantly changing with current and tidal activity depending on various oceanographic conditions. Fishermen have to carefully steam through a "gully" to get to open sea before heading to their fishing grounds. They were aware that the channel had narrowed over the winter, and several fishermen, including Ian Benoit, had advocated vigorously for speedy action to have the channel widened by dredging, to make it safer for vessels heading to sea.

Fisheries and Oceans Canada said it had been working on a plan with local fishermen since the fall of 2012 to dredge an access channel. In a statement issued in late May, DFO said "sounding" surveys were conducted on April 22 and May 7, after which the department requested the proper permits from Environment Canada to proceed with dredging.

"The geographic location and the tidal currents of McEachern's Point naturally encourage sedimentation. The access channel has shifted 250 metres south from its position last year," the DFO statement said.

It wasn't stormy, but weather had been unsettled near Tabusintac on May 16 and 17, 2013. Northeast winds and moderate seas made fishing a little uncomfortable but not bad enough to remain in port. Similar conditions continued into Saturday, May 18.

As fishermen gathered at the McEachern's Point wharf early Saturday morning to prepare for fishing, the captains sized up the skies, wind direction and speed, and tide and wave conditions offshore before making a decision to untie. Some decided to wait until after daylight, but most, including Weldon Harding and Ian Benoit, thought it would be fine to leave before dawn. Weldon says the weather was fair enough for fishing, and with the tide rising they should be able to navigate the "Gut" without a problem. In fact, they reasoned, coming back later that day should be better, with higher tides, even if the winds breezed up a little higher.

"The forecast said the wind was expected to pick up by noon, but we figured that we'd get half or three quarters of a trip in, and if it looked like it was gonna get bad, we'd come in," Weldon recalls. So, for most boats it was a go.

Weldon says he was the third or fourth boat to head out in the dark.

"There was a bit of sea on, so we kept spottin' the buoys [with spot-lights] as we went and it wasn't too bad, but when I was about at the end [of the Gully], a couple of waves hit us and then I took a pretty good one right on the side of her and I thought, 'Geez, that's funny,' because it didn't look that bad in the spotlight, but we had a new gully cut through the sand [by sedimentation] just above the old one in the past few days. Sand can move that quick, and it looked like the two of them were kind of filling in and probably meeting together at the end," he says, explaining that the shifting sands and new gullies created by nature's forces probably created unpredictable wave action.

Weldon and his crew made it through the gully and kept on steaming, but the farther he went the rougher it got, so he started wondering whether it was wise to proceed.

"So, I called my buddy Jamie, who was up ahead of me, and asked where he was. He said, 'I'm about ten miles off,' so I asked him what it was like and he said he was only doing about four or five knots. I said to him, 'You have another five miles to go and I have about ten, so that's gonna take you another hour and me two,' so I said to hell with this, I'm goin' back home."

A short while later, Ian Benoit called Weldon and, after a few minutes, several skippers, including Ian and his twin brother, Eric Benoit, who was on a different boat, got in touch again and exchanged opinions on what to do.

"Ian asked what I was going to do and I said, 'I'm going back but I'm gonna wait till daylight before trying to get through that bloody hole [gully], because it was kinda dirty when we came through on the way out. Ian said yeah, it seemed to be a good idea, so the three of us, Ian and his brother Eric and me, turned around and headed back."

Both Ian and Eric had been behind Weldon on the way out, but now they were ahead of him, going back, so he kept a close eye on both the Benoit boats along the way while at the same time trying to hang back a little more and wait for daylight.

As they got closer to the sandbars and in shallower water, seas got considerably rougher. By the time the three boats were approaching the entrance to the gully, Weldon saw a couple of big waves strike both the boats that were less than a quarter-mile in front of him.

"A couple of minutes later, all hell broke loose," Weldon says.

Captain Weldon Harding was keeping a very close eye on the two boats just a few hundred yards ahead of him as they approached the so-called "gully" leading through the sandbars to get back home to Tabusintac. Thirty-five-year-old twin brothers Ian and Eric Benoit, captains of separate vessels, were approaching the most vulnerable area of the gully while Weldon hung behind his friends a little bit, intending to wait for more daylight to improve his chances for a successful passage through the narrow gully. A veteran skipper, Weldon said seas were running strong and erratic in the shallow waters.

"I saw a couple of big waves, and then one real big wave that struck Eric, and suddenly he was nowhere to be seen for a little while. And then I saw Ian, who was now in the gully, and I saw the waves coming at him, too, and after the third one, I'm there going, 'Now's your chance, boys, now's your chance!' Usually they [waves] come in threes and then you get a little lull, so I was there goin', 'Give 'er, give 'er, give 'er, now's your chance,' and he was doing everything right. With the third one, he was riding it with the bow up on it, but after the third one, out of the blue came this big one, a surprise fourth one, and struck Ian right on the side, laid right into the side of her, rolled her out—you could see her keel. He must have seen it coming because he tried to cut her to take it on an angle and ride it, but it was too late, and when she came down off the wave, she came down fast and she came down arse first, and he was thrown all the way over on the other side of the gully, and then I knew he was in bad trouble!"

"Trouble" meant that Ian's boat had been tossed onto the sandbar and was hard aground. Weldon says he wasn't sure what to do, but he knew he had to try to save his friend Ian along with his two deckhands, Samuel René Boutin, just twenty-three years of age, from Saumarez, and Alfred Rousselle, age thirty-two of nearby Brantville.

Ian's brother, Eric, was thinking the same thing. Both captains tried to manoeuvre their vessels closer to Ian's boat, but as much as they

Captain Weldon Harding at wheelhouse door (Photo courtesy of Gail Harding)

wanted to rescue Ian and his crew, both skippers were aware that getting close enough to get a line to Ian's boat would seriously jeopardize themselves and their own crews—instead of one boat stranded in pounding seas, there would be two or three in the same predicament with no hope of rescue. On one occasion, Weldon's boat was hit by a wave with such force that he was knocked off balance and wound up flat on his back on the wheelhouse floor.

"I called Eric and said if we try and go in there too close we're gonna be in the same damn mess the boys are in—but as long as she stays there [on the bar] with bow to the seas, it might be okay. So, I called 911 and said that we needed a Zodiac out here," Weldon recalls.

But Ian's boat didn't stay put. Each series of waves that pounded against the vessel turned it more and more until finally she had

Charred remains of some of the burnt vessels (Photo courtesy of Gail Harding)

swivelled with the stern to the seas, and that marked the beginning of the end. Now, seas were washing over the stern and swamping the vessel.

It was a frustrating and emotionally charged time for Eric and Weldon. Ian had been a crew member with Weldon for eight years.

"He was like a son to me and Genevieve," Weldon muses sadly. "I suppose they were praying that we could get to them, and I was praying that I could get to them, too. But you can only go so far—I mean, every time we tried to get closer, we were scrapin' bottom, too, and the tide was falling."

As for Eric, watching his twin brother and crew being battered by heavy seas, aground on a sandbar, entirely at the mercy of an unforgiving ocean, was the worst scene he had ever witnessed. Eric's sense of helplessness was almost unbearable.

In a media interview, Eric said, "I saw the boat on the bar filling with water and I saw two men on top of the wheelhouse and [knowing] we couldn't do anything for them—it was too late."

Weldon also saw two men on top of the boat, one clinging to the column risers, but he couldn't tell who was who. In fact, at the time, Weldon wasn't even sure whether there had been two or three men on board Ian's boat.

"Once, I did get close enough, maybe a hundred yards or whatever, but close enough to know it was Alfred, because that time I got close enough that he made it to the bow and grabbed the line hoping that I could get close enough that he could throw it to me—but all I ever saw was two men, so I think that one of them, I don't know if it was Ian or not, was thrown over when the boat took that dive and hit the bar."

Any hope of rescue was quickly fading, although word had spread to other skippers in Tabusintac and several other vessels had arrived on the scene to offer whatever assistance they could. But no matter how many boats were on hand, there was nothing any of them could do. It was impossible to get close to the stranded vessel.

"Every time we'd go in to take another look, Ian's boat was getting lower and lower in the water, so obviously she was taking on water pretty fast. And then the last time I went in, she was nowhere to be seen."

Weldon explains that there was an area of deeper water next to the bar where Ian's boat had grounded, so it had obviously slid from the bar and into that "hole," as Weldon describes it.

Given the conditions of the sea, the weather, and their intimate knowledge of the sandbars and waters surrounding them, all the captains knew they were no longer on a rescue mission. The next task was going to be a search for bodies.

Rescuers discovered the body of René Boutin on Saturday afternoon. Ian Benoit and Samuel Rousselle were found the next day. According to Weldon's estimates, all three bodies were discovered about two and a half to three miles away from where the vessel sank.

The loss of three young fishermen from the Tabusintac region left people shaken for reasons that go beyond the usual grief with such a sad loss.

Many people felt the tragedy could have been avoided if government had only paid more attention to fishermen like Ian Benoit, who had advocated strongly to authorities to work with fishermen and find a better system to monitor and dredge the ever-shifting sands on the bottom of the ocean in his area. Weldon Harding says that sand moves and creates sandbars similar to the way drifting snow swirls around, creating high snowbanks in one location, and leaves bare ground a few feet away.

For that reason, some people say they still have a rage burning inside them because of this accident. Weldon Harding, a veteran skipper who' has seen a lot in his many years on the water, says he's lost his enthusiasm and love for the fishing industry.

"It just won't be the same anymore," he says.

CHAPTER 7

The Woodmans of New Harbour

Fred Woodman Jr. is not shy and he loves to talk. The semi-retired fish processor from New Harbour, Trinity Bay, on the east coast of Newfoundland, leaves no doubt about his opinion on any issue.

The fifty-three-year-old avid outdoorsman grew up in a family that talked fish from daylight to dark nearly every day.

Fred is the son of parents who promoted lively discussion and debate. Fred Woodman Sr. and his wife, Cairine, never held back on expressing their

Fred Woodman Jr.

opinions, especially about the fishing industry, because both were owners of Woodman Fisheries, the fish company that Fred Jr. along with his brother Geoff eventually wound up owning.

Former Woodman plant on north side of New Harbour, Trinity Bay

Fred Sr. never backed away from an argument and had no time for fence-sitting, either, in his personal life or in business.

"I remember Dad wanting to finalize issues and he'd say, 'Make a damn decision—even if it's a bad decision—at least make one,'" Fred Jr. recalls.

Fred Sr. dabbled in capital "P" politics for a few years, having run unsuccessfully for the PC Party both provincially and federally. He also served on the board of nearly every fisheries committee and organization that ever existed in Canada.

Despite his father's high profile, Fred Jr. points out that he was owner of the family business longer than his dad.

"People thought that Dad was always the owner because he was so visible and high-profile. People just assumed he still owned and operated the company," he said.

Former Woodman plant on south side of New Harbour, Trinity Bay

In fact, Fred Jr. made a lease-to-buy arrangement with his father back in 1985 in a seven-year package. Fred laughs heartily about it now, but it was no laughing matter when the seven years were up and the time came to take it to the next level.

It was 1992, the year when cod was placed under moratorium.

"So here I was, after spending $750,000 or more upgrading and expanding a groundfish plant and buying other companies and everything else, and then suddenly there was no cod to be had," he said.

Fred says they managed to survive through complex purchases of Russian cod and scrounging up a few tons of fish wherever they could.

"Then in 1994, we got a little break—the Japanese wanted as much caplin as they could get their hands on and were paying good money for it, and we just happened to have had a good caplin fishery that year and that's what saved us for a couple more years."

But it was a struggle until, finally, Woodman Sea Products was granted a crab licence in 1997 and the company sailed into financially calmer waters.

By the time Fred Jr. turned fifty, he'd grown weary of the fish business. After the demise of cod, it was never the same, he says. The industry seemed to lurch from one direction to another like a ship without a rudder and there was no longer any cohesiveness in the industry.

"Everyone is frightened to death to offer an idea these days, because the minute you fly it they're out there waiting to shoot it down—sometimes just for the sake of shooting it down, no matter how good and honest the idea is," he says.

Fred says he misses the days of cod when hundreds of people worked at the plant and the wheels of industry hummed along at a relatively steady pace, and if fishermen and processors worked hard, everyone could make a living.

But everything changed after the moratorium. It was as if the industry's heartbeat had been stilled. So, in 2010, when Daley Brothers were looking to buy a plant, Fred was interested in talking.

"After all, it's not every day that someone comes along and wants to talk about buying your fish business these days," he says. Fred and Daleys made a deal. Meanwhile, both Fred and Geoff are still involved on a contract basis.

"I still deal with my fishermen and my traditional buyers, like the Japanese and so on."

Daleys have invested further into the New Harbour operation, and that makes Fred very happy.

"I would not have sold if I thought the buyer was planning to move the business out of the community. I want to always hear the sound of forklifts, air compressors, and trucks forever in New Harbour. That is extremely important to me and that is why Daleys' offer was attractive to me. I knew they intended to invest in the New Harbour plant."

A conversation with Fred Woodman about anything these days usually segues to his lifelong passion: hunting. And now that he has more time to indulge in that passion, he spends more time than ever in the woods. He recently returned from Saskatchewan, where he was guiding a hunting expedition for a month.

"Hunting is the only thing and place in the world where I am totally at peace," he says with a smile. "I hunt like I'm hungry. When I'm out there in the morning chasing a bird or something, I hunt like I won't have anything for supper unless I'm successful. I eat, breathe, and sleep hunting twenty-four hours a day, 365 days a year." He has also turned photography into a bit of a hobby and has an artistic eye. He is keenly aware when he sees what will be a good photo.

Fred has many stories about growing up in New Harbour as the son of a businessman. In small-town Newfoundland, class distinction has always been polarized between fisherman and the so-called merchant. From the days of the Water Street merchants of St. John's, fish processors are often vilified as conniving and bad people. Fred says he remembers being told to leave a friend's house simply because he was the son of a fish processor.

"That kind of stuff is hard to understand when you're only six or seven years old."

Perhaps that's why his mom might have preferred that her sons had followed a different career path. Even though Fred sensed her feelings, she didn't try to change his mind. Fred says his family worked very hard in the family business.

"It was daylight till dark, and the first one home would make something for supper because Mother was often the last one to leave the plant," he recalled.

Fred's outgoing personality and joy of living probably helped him deal with the negativity of small-town politics. He truly enjoyed being able to offer jobs to people in his community.

"I'd say that as many as ninety-five per cent of the working people in New Harbour area worked for us at one time or another."

Conversely, he says it was very painful when he had to let someone go.

"That person was probably a neighbour or a family friend, because in a small town everyone is your neighbour."

Fred Woodman Jr. is a content person these days. His dad passed away, but even when Fred Sr. was ailing, Fred Jr. would drop by as often as he could for a visit and took his dad for a drive and a chat.

"We were very much alike, and that's probably why we argued so much. There were times we'd almost come to smacks at the plant, and on the way home for supper Dad would say 'I guess we won't go troutin' this evening, then.' 'Oh yes, sure we will, I'll pick you up at six thirty,' I'd reply, and that would be the end of that."

Fred Jr. says his father had ample opportunity to rub his nose in the dirt for making a bad deal once or twice, but he never did. It's about respect, he says.

"One time I really screwed up on a deal and Dad looked at me and said, 'I guess some people have to go to university for five years to learn something, but I think you learned a good lesson this time.'

"'Lesson learned, Dad,' I said. And you know what? Of all the things I can think about now, what I remember most is that he never made anything of it."

Perhaps Fred Sr. remembered his own advice. "Make a decision, even if it's a bad one."

CHAPTER 8

Privateers and Cutthroats

"Rosborough" was an instantly recognizable brand in the world of wooden yachts from the 1960s through to the age of fibreglass boats.

Rosborough was James "Doug" Rosborough from Halifax, the designer of nearly 150 distinctive yachts for a host of clients that included some of North America's most prominent people.

Doug developed a deep love of boats when he was just a boy. His business career began with a fascination for the lowly little schooners known as "jack boats" that were popular on the south coast of Newfoundland.

Doug's business plan was simple: find an old Newfoundland jack schooner that was destined to be chopped up for firewood and bring it to Nova Scotia for rebuilding and put a "For Sale" sign on it.

In the pursuit of growing a business in the marine industry, oftentimes the people one must associate with are not all members of the church choir. Doug learned all about that when he needed to hire people to sail boats from Newfoundland to Nova Scotia. Finding a crew was not always easy and he'd often be forced to settle for old salts of dubious character.

In his memoir, a wonderful book called *Confessions of a Boatbuilder*, Doug recounts a story when one of his clients couldn't wait to see his future boat even before it had been refurbished and converted to a pleasure craft.

An American fellow named Sid Rice drove his big yellow Cadillac up from the United States, picked up Doug, and drove to the wharf where Doug's motley crew of rogues had docked for the night.

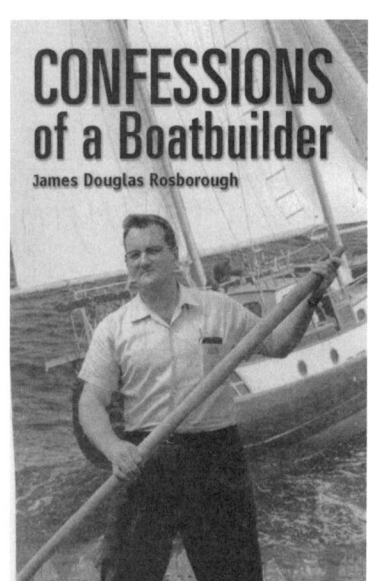

Cover of Doug Rosborough's autobiography *Confessions of a Boatbuilder* (Photo courtesy of Bob Rosborough)

"I tooted the horn [on Sid's Cadillac] and three bedraggled, hungover heads appeared out of the schooner hatches. One was Don Holder, with stubble beard and a battered hat, while another was one-eyed Eddie who had lost an eye in a barroom brawl and only the sunken socket remained. The third was Captain Tom McMartin with long hair, a huge gold earring, and a two-foot-long sheath knife on his belt.

"Oh my God, look at them!" Sid exclaimed. "Captain Blood and his Calcutta Cutthroats."

After several years buying, redesigning, and rebuilding old schooners, a shipyard owner and friend sat Doug down for a chat one day.

"Cyril Russell insisted that it would be far less frustrating and easier to build new boats than to repair old ones—and went on to explain why," Doug says.

He respected Cyril and valued his opinion, and after some initial reluctance he decided he would study new vessel design and give it a try. Doug, married with children, also worked with the telephone company full-time to make ends meet and couldn't go back to the classroom, so he bought all the instructional material he could find and studied every word.

"Dad is a self-made man," Doug's eldest son, Bob Rosborough, explains. "He is a vessel designer-constructor," he says, with heavy emphasis on the *tor*. Doug also liked to refer to himself by using that old-fashioned term.

"Traditionally, a 'constructor' designed the vessel, took his plans to the yard, and often lived there to interpret his design and the owner's wishes," Doug says, giving his reader-listener the feeling that he took great pride in being that person.

After reaching his self-applied competence and comfort level in new design, Doug was ready for his new career and it wasn't long before orders were coming in. Doug hired shipyards in Ship Harbour, Chester, Sambro, and eventually A. F. Theriault Ltd. in Meteghan to carry out his construction work, and soon he knew every yard employee and everything about them.

While the builders were not as colourful as the sailors, some were "interesting," to put it politely. After being greeted one morning with a gruff grumble from one fellow, Doug was informed by a co-worker that this was not a good day to ask how the builder's day was going.

"His wife left him a few days ago, he just had a fight with his daughter, and she left, too. The mortgage company seized his house and the sheriff seized the boat shop. A neighbour complained that his German shepherd had broken a chain and went over and killed several of the neighbour's chickens, so he borrowed someone's gun and shot the dog. So, Doug, boy, this was not a good time to ask how his day was going."

Bob Rosborough sitting in one of the company's current small-boat designs

Doug's early love of basic schooner design influenced his work and resulted in sailing yachts of various descriptions, mostly brigantines. Privateers were his specialty. He also did several modern powerboats, but the golden age of sail was his first love. One of his most complex brigs was built for Admiral Richard Black of the US Navy.

Admiral Black had great knowledge of ships and knew exactly what he wanted, so the construction of his forty-six-foot vessel *Valkyrie* was very much a custom design. Black had acquired some oak wood from the famous USS *Constitution*, a three-masted, wooden, heavy frigate built in the late 1790s. The admiral wanted to use the oak to fashion gun carriages for a small, but working, cannon to be mounted on his vessel. In keeping with his desire to have his yacht as authentic as possible to the colonial period that he knew so much about, Admiral Black had Doug design and cast one-inch swivel guns to be mounted on the "taffrails" aft.

Rosborough wooden vessels under construction
at A. F. Theriault's Shipyard in Meteghan, Nova Scotia

Clearly, Doug immensely enjoyed his new friend, who, by Doug's own description, was captivating as he told endless spellbinding tales. Among other accomplishments, a young Richard Black sailed with Rear Admiral Richard E. Byrd on several of the more famous admiral's Antarctic expeditions. Doug took great pride in building for Admiral Black the private vessel of his dreams.

Doug Rosborough was a hard worker and every vessel he designed was a work of art, built with integrity and great craftsmanship. Although a couple of unscrupulous buyers stiffed him on final payments, it was never because of shoddy work. It was because they were shysters of the first order who took advantage of an honest man who did most contracts based on nothing more than a handshake.

A line in his book discussed what he came to know as the difference between Canadians and Americans. He said when things went wrong, Canadians asked how to fix the problem. Americans asked: "Who do we blame and sue?"

But still, most of Doug's business was done for clients south of the border and the vast majority were good to deal with.

Rosborough's business peaked around 1970. In 1973, he had fifteen boats under construction in five yards. Life was good. But dark clouds were building on the wooden boat horizon with the promise of strong headwinds.

In the 1980s, fibreglass was suddenly the rage. Because fibre was lighter, durable, and less expensive than wood, fishermen, government agencies, and other clients were switching. Fortunately, Bob Rosborough had been working with his father long enough to know the company well. Bob adapted easily to the new-age demand. He had a keen sense of business and, because he worked at sea with the Bedford Institute of Oceanography for several years, he was well-equipped to lead the company on a new tack.

For Doug, steeped in the culture of wood and sail all those years, adapting was not so easy. The thought that no one wanted wooden boats anymore was difficult to accept. In 1990, he was forced to come to terms with an uncertain future. His life of adventure and swashbuckling friends had suddenly gone quiet. To add to his confusion, his thirty-five-year marriage ended at the same time.

"It was all mystifying to me. I couldn't understand, the bottom had dropped out of my world—it was the dark night of my soul and I didn't know what to do," he wrote.

Doug retreated to the family cottage in the woods at Lake Charlotte, where he lived for a couple of years. He ultimately figured things out and lived a happier life in retirement with his endless memories, photos, ships plans, and stories.

Rosborough Boats continues as a strong and distinctive boatbuilding company under Bob's leadership and with the able assistance of another Rosborough, Bob's son Heaton.

Doug still has plenty of reason to be proud.

CHAPTER 9

Hodges Cove Black Christmas

Christmas 1976 was shaping up to be the usual season of holiday merriment for the small Trinity Bay community of Hodges Cove, located about a two-hour drive northwest of St. John's.

In fact, for the family of twenty-one-year-old Willis Thomas, it was going to be an extra special Christmas. Willis had been working in Labrador City for the previous four years and this was going to be his first Christmas home since he started working up north.

But there was another reason for celebration that year—Willis was also home to become engaged. The wedding was to take place a month later. His fiancée was three months pregnant, with their baby expected to arrive in late spring 1977.

In an interview with CBC's *Land and Sea* program, Willis's sister, Patsy, said the whole family was excited about having her brother home, and with the engagement and upcoming wedding planning, this would be a Christmas like none other.

Patsy was right—it would be a Christmas like no other. But not the joyous occasion she had expected.

Willis's dad, Cyril Thomas, loved a game of cards, and on Thursday night, December 23, several men gathered at the Thomas household for a chat and a few hands of cards. Willis was one of them. His friend Hedley Drover was another, along with Hedley's good friend Wes "Willis" Peddle.

Late in the evening, Willis decided to open a bottle of rum to offer a drink to his father and friends.

"It's handy enough to Christmas to have a little drink now, boys. You never know if we'll ever get the chance to have another one together again," Willis said.

While sipping their drinks, Hedley mentioned that he might "go across the Arm to Mooring Cove" and check his cod net the next morning. Wes suggested that he would probably join him and perhaps they could also have a look at Wes's herring net while they were out there. Willis, who was always there to lend a helping hand, said that he'd like to go with his friends, and he invited them to go in his small speedboat.

When Wes Peddle looked out his window on Christmas Eve morning, he changed his mind about going out in boat that day. It was a grey, overcast, damp morning with fairly strong winds and occasional drizzle. He assumed that Hedley wouldn't bother checking on his cod net because it would not be comfortable in a small sixteen-foot open boat. Wes told his wife, Audrey, that he would go in the woods and cut some firewood instead.

Unlike Wes, forty-five-year-old Hedley Drover was not deterred by the weather conditions that morning.

Christmas was traditionally a time of community visiting in rural Newfoundland communities, and no visit would be complete unless the host offered a snack to his or her guests. Not only that, several of Hedley's nine children were still living at home, and with a family to feed every day, along with expected company during the Christmas holiday season, a few dozen codfish fillets in the freezer would make things a lot nicer for the season's festivities at the Drover household.

Still, Hedley didn't appear to be in a hurry to leave Hodges Cove to go to his net that Christmas Eve morning. His son Dennis remembers Hedley splitting firewood and bringing it in the house to dry.

Dennis was a typical eleven-year-old boy who loved a game of hockey. He recalls that he was rounding up hockey sticks and other

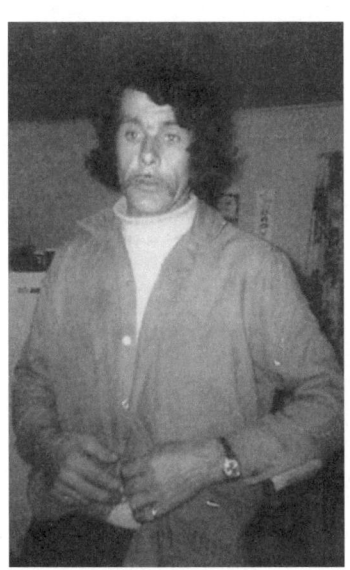

Hedley Drover

things to have a game of street hockey with his buddies on the wharf not far from their house. Like all children his age, Dennis was full of wonderment and excitement about the anticipated Christmas presents that would be under the tree the next morning. Perhaps there might be a piece of hockey equipment or, if he was really lucky, the Mastermind game he'd asked Santa for that year.

But that Christmas morning would not be a time for opening gifts in the Drover household.

When Hedley finished chopping wood, he contacted his young friend Willis Thomas to see if Willis's offer to join him in checking his cod nets still stood. Willis agreed and again suggested they could go in his little speedboat. The two men later met at the beach, and after deciding that the wind and seas were still not too bad, the two men prepared to go across Southwest Arm to haul Hedley's two gillnets at Mooring Cove Point. After all, it was only a mile across the Arm and they would be back home again in an hour.

Like Willis Thomas, Cal "Calvin" Drover also worked in Labrador City in 1976 and he, too, was home in Hodges Cove to spend Christmas with his dad, Hedley, and mom, Beulah, along with several siblings and other family members.

Cal remembers being on the beach when his dad and Willis climbed into the small boat. In fact, Willis tried coaxing Cal into joining them.

"He was saying, 'Come on, Cal, we won't be long,' but I didn't feel like going and said I'd probably go in the woods and get some wood for Christmas," Cal recalled.

Willis Thomas

"Nah, come on, we'll be back in a little while, and then tonight we'll have a few drinks," Willis implored.

But Cal had his mind made up. He wasn't going out in boat that morning.

"Okay then, if you're not comin', then shove us off, will you," Hedley said to his son.

Cal obliged and pushed the small boat away from the beach and looked at his father as the two men set out to haul the net.

Cal would be the last person to see to his dad and Willis alive.

Back in Hodges Cove, everything was proceeding as any other Christmas Eve. Women were baking cookies and treats and putting the last touches on the household decorations for the holiday season. Men were working on getting firewood and putting up the last strings of outdoor Christmas lights.

By midday, several hours after Willis and Hedley said they would be back home, the winds had significantly increased and concerns about the two men started to grow. Hedley's wife, Beulah, kept glancing out her pantry window to see if there was any sign of a speedboat coming in the small harbour.

Her anxiety increasing with every passing minute, Beulah went to the Thomas residence to see if they had heard from Willis. Willis's mother, Ethel Thomas, said she hadn't heard anything from her son and mentioned that she, too, was getting worried. Both women then decided to contact other people to see if anyone knew anything about Willis and Hedley's whereabouts. One of them was Peddle.

Wes didn't share the women's fear at first.

When he came home from the woods about noon, his wife, Audrey, mentioned that Hedley and Willis had gone out in boat and were overdue. Wes knew Hedley very well and suggested that his friend probably went to nearby Hatchet Cove after hauling his nets and was likely enjoying a Christmas Eve drink with friends there.

By early afternoon, Beulah couldn't look out the window any longer. She had to do something. She called and asked Wes if he would consider going across the Arm to see if there was any sign of her husband and Willis. It was windy and seas were getting rough, but Wes said he would take a look.

Wes Peddle contacted his friend Walter Drover and told him what was going on. Walter said he would go with Wes, and a few minutes later the two men ventured out from Hodges Cove in Walt's boat to search for Willis and Hedley.

The morning showers had turned into a steady rainfall accompanied by a strong southeasterly wind, so "Uncle" Walt, as he was known to Wes and most others, decided to go to a nearby community to top up his fuel tank in case they ran into conditions that would mean taking longer than expected to get back home.

Coming out of Hatchet Cove, they narrowly escaped being added to the list of missing persons themselves that afternoon.

"We nearly capsized," Wes says, explaining that a couple of large waves nearly tossed their boat bow over stern.

Uncle Walt was back aft on the motor, so Wes quickly moved forward, from where he was sitting in the middle of the boat, to the front to provide more weight in the bow. That would help stabilize the vessel until Walt could manoeuvre the speedboat to a better angle against the seas and wind. What Wes calls "a bit of a fright" was enough to convince the two men that it was too dangerous to continue searching for their two friends, so they decided to guide the boat, cautiously, through the rough seas back to Hodges Cove.

With Wes and Uncle Walt's arrival back home, fears for the two missing men heightened. Uncle Walt's boat was a sturdy eighteen-foot speedboat with a twenty-horsepower engine, and if that one almost capsized, how could a smaller, sixteen-foot punt speedboat survive in those conditions?

Hodges Cove's black Christmas started that evening—literally. While an entire community waited and worried, hardly anyone felt festive enough to turn on Christmas lights. The small Trinity Bay town looked like any other dreary night in winter, not the normally brightly lit and happy place on Christmas Eve.

Dennis Drover

Dennis Drover still gets emotional when he talks about the events of Christmas 1976.

At eleven years of age, he was old enough to understand from the sombre and anxious conversations of the adults that something was terribly wrong. Although thirty-six years have passed, tears still well up when Dennis recalls when the younger Drover children were preparing for bed that night. What was supposed to be a night of wide-eyed excitement, waiting for morning's first light to see what Santa Claus would bring, had turned into a sickening feeling that was all-consuming for Dennis.

His younger sister Lisa, who was just nine, asked Dennis if he thought their dad and Willis were going to be all right. It was Christmas Eve and Dennis wanted to say something positive to calm his little sister's fears, but even though he tried, the proper words were hard to find because his mind was in such turmoil that talking about his dad was almost impossible.

"I'll never forget that moment as long as I live," Dennis says softly, his voice trembling with raw emotion.

At dawn on Christmas morning, nearly every man in Hodges Cove was on the beach preparing to untie his boat and search for Hedley and

Willis. Among them were Wes and Uncle Walt. The winds had abated considerably overnight and the rain had stopped. The cresting seas had also subsided, but there was still a fairly large sea swell running after the bad weather on Christmas Eve.

"It was a fair day," Wes summed it up.

Just as he and Walt were about to leave Hodges Cove, Cyril Stringer stopped by to ask if he could join them.

"Uncle Walt asked Cyril if he was sure about that, because Cyril was Willis Thomas's first cousin as well as a close friend, and Uncle Walt worried that, if the worst happened, Cyril might be affected or something," Wes remembers.

But Cyril insisted that he would be fine no matter what and that he really wanted to help.

Boats of various sizes and descriptions—speedboats, longliners, and pleasure craft—were soon steaming across Southwest Arm on Christmas morning. While everyone on the boats and back home in Hodges Cove homes prayed that Hedley Drover and Willis Thomas would be found alive and well, there was a pall of dread hanging over them.

"We went across the Arm to the Hatchet Cove area first and then worked our way back down the shore from there," Wes explains. "When we got down a bit farther, someone called out from another boat that there was a half-sunk speedboat stuck in a crevice in the rocks. So Uncle Walt got our boat as close to the rocks as he could—there was a big swell—and I jumped and Cyril jumped and we ran down around the rocks to where the boat was, and when we got down a bit closer I could see this black thing lying in the bottom of the boat."

At first Wes was convinced that the "black thing" was a body, but as he slowly walked closer he realized that it was Willis's black Mercury outboard motor. There was no sign of Willis or Hedley.

With this new development, Uncle Walt, Wes, and Cyril got together with several of the men in the other boats and discussed what to do next. Wes and Cyril made several observations that proved relevant to what might have happened to Hedley and Willis. Those observations provided guidance for the steps to follow.

The first observation was that the men had time to remove the engine from the boat's counter and place it on the bottom of the small speedboat. That told them it wasn't a hard collision against the rocks. Secondly, the boat was intact but for one exception. A piece of the boat's planking toward the bow had been punctured. Also, the cap belonging to the gas can was still in the boat, but the tank itself was nowhere to be seen. For seasoned fishermen and men who practically grew up on the water in Newfoundland, that second observation offered a glimmer of hope in their initial homespun investigation.

In the days when life jackets were hardly ever found on board small boats, the searchers knew that an empty gas tank was sometimes used as a flotation device when vessels sank. Hedley could swim and Willis was an excellent swimmer, so Uncle Walt and the others determined that if the two men managed to get out of the boat and away from the slippery freezing rocks alive, and then cling to the empty gas can for buoyancy, it just might be possible they made it to a beach and safety.

Somewhat encouraged by this development, and knowing that Hedley, particularly, was a very experienced woodsman, the searchers dared to hope that the two missing men had made it to shore and had walked into the woods. Hedley would have known that there was a road not far beyond their location that could take him toward Hatchet Cove not far away.

With all those factors in mind, the men decided that they would go back to Hodges Cove and contact the RCMP to see if there was a tracking dog available to conduct a land search. The others would stay in the vicinity of where Willis's boat was found and continue to search the shoreline.

As Wes Peddle and Uncle Walt Drover headed back to Hodges Cove to contact the RCMP, other boats continued searching in the vicinity of Mooring Cove on Christmas Day where Willis's little speedboat was found half-submerged.

When Wes and Uncle Walt arrived back in their community, they contacted the RCMP with an update on finding Willis's punt. During the conversation, Wes explained that because both Hedley and Willis could swim, it was possible they had made it to shore and tried walking to safety. Hedley was an experienced hunter and woodsman, and if he made it to shore, Wes and Uncle Walt reasoned that the two would have a good chance at surviving, even in winter. Wes asked the officer if he would consider getting a tracking dog and searching the area of woods in the vicinity where the boat was found.

The officer agreed and said he'd be along shortly. Approximately a half-hour later, Wes met the policeman on the beach in Hodges Cove and continued to discuss strategy for a search.

"But all of a sudden I noticed that some boats were leaving Mooring Cove and coming across the Arm, and I looked at the cop and said, 'Hang on a minute, there's a couple of boats headed this way, and they wouldn't be doing that unless there's something going on.'"

Sure enough, he was right—there was a new development and it was not good news. Wes's father-in-law, Azariah King, arrived at the wharf in his thirty-five-foot longliner and announced that they had found Willis's body. He later explained that searchers were scouring the waters off Mooring Cove Point when someone saw something yellow on the bottom, about seven or eight feet underwater. It was Willis in his yellow rubber clothes in a kneeling position. It looked as if he had been trying to crawl along the rocky ledge to the surface but couldn't make it. One of the men lowered a cod jigger and retrieved the body.

During the course of getting the update from Azariah, the police officer asked Wes if he thought they should go and search for Hedley.

"I looked out and saw all the boats coming toward us, and I knew then that they had found Hedley," Wes says. "I looked at the officer and told him that no, there would be no need for us to look for Hedley because they have him—the men in those boats would not all be coming home otherwise."

A few minutes later, the first of the boats arrived with the sad news that they had indeed found Hedley's body in Mooring Cove, half in the water and half on the beach. An empty gas tank was also found nearby.

Meanwhile, eleven-year-old Dennis Drover was struggling with how to deal with everything that Christmas morning.

"I got up and there were people everywhere. I still had that sick feeling from the night before and could hear some of what they were saying and I couldn't stand it. I just had to get away from there. So, I took my skates and hockey stick and left and went to one of my friends', but his house was up on a bank that overlooked the harbour where you could see everything going on down there and I didn't want to see that, so I went to another friend's place. My friend's mom told me to come in and that she'd get me some breakfast. Later, my friend's father said he'd go and see if there was any news. A little while later, he came back and took my friend and me to a back room in the house where he sat me down and he told me they had found my father's body."

Dennis still gets overwhelmed with emotion when he remembers that day. Sitting alongside his wife, Allison, in the *Navigator* office in July 2013, it was difficult for him to talk about it. Composing himself as much as he could, he talked about his reaction after being told on Christmas Day that his dad was dead.

Mooring Cove, Southwest Arm, the location where both bodies were found

"I don't know what I was thinking, to be honest, but I had to do something. I remember taking my hockey stuff and skates and I went in on the pond and played hockey until I finally realized that I had to go home."

After that, many of the hours and even days are somewhat blurred for Dennis. He knew he couldn't bring himself to go to the funeral. He withdrew into his own personal space for some time. In fact, that withdrawal has lasted, to some extent, for years.

Dennis was just one of many Hodges Cove people who had to deal with a broken heart that Christmas. The Drover and Thomas families included dozens of immediate family members—children, siblings, parents, cousins. And of course, as in all small rural Newfoundland and Labrador communities, neighbours and friends were, more or less, extended family.

Willis Thomas's brother Doug was working in Labrador City that year, as were several members of both the Thomas and Drover families. Their relatives back home on the island decided to keep the news that Hedley and Willis were missing away from them at first. After all, it was Christmas Eve and everyone thought there would be a good chance to find both missing men alive and well on Christmas Day, so there was no need to get everyone who was away from home upset on this special day. But there was no way to hide the awful truth once Christmas Day came.

"I was home on Christmas Day," says Doug, who is a few years older than his brother Willis. "We had children who were doing the usual stuff that children do when they have new presents and so on, and sometime in the afternoon I saw the clergyman's car coming in the driveway, and of course you know when you see the minister coming to your door like that, it usually means something is wrong."

Back in Hodges Cove, Wes Peddle says, the community looked and felt like it died, too. "There was no life, no nothing. The funeral went as well as could be expected, I suppose, but it was like everyone was just going through the motions. Nobody turned on any Christmas lights—it was literally a black Christmas," Wes says, staring at the floor.

"But then, about six days into Christmas, Uncle Cyril, Willis's father, called me and said 'Wes, can you do something for me?' 'Sure,

Uncle Cyril,' I said, 'anything.' 'How about turning on your Christmas lights? Willis would want that, especially for the children.'"

Wes flicked a light switch and turned on his Christmas lights. A few minutes later, another house was lit, and then another and another, until soon Hodges Cove looked like it had suddenly started breathing again.

When fishermen and others from small rural communities die young and suddenly, families are often left with severe hardship. Long after the normal grieving period passes, mere survival for many families is extremely difficult. In the Hodges Cove tragedy, Willis Thomas left his mom and dad, along with six siblings, but he also left behind his common-law wife, Lorraine Pitcher, who was expecting their child the following spring. How would she cope? Hedley Drover left his wife and nine children, several of whom were still living at home. Without employment to provide an income, his widow, Beulah, faced a very scary future.

In June 1977, Lorraine gave birth to a beautiful daughter. Without Willis in her life, Lorraine, who was still a very young woman, was overwhelmed by the thoughts of raising a child on her own. Willis's brother Ron and his wife offered to adopt Lori, the baby, which everyone agreed was a wonderful idea. That way the child would grow up in a good home and still be in the Thomas family. Now in her thirties, Lori is also a mom, living in Labrador City.

Beulah Drover was also distraught and overwhelmed facing an uncertain future without her husband. In a state of high anxiety, worried about coping, Beulah accepted her son Carson's invitation to spend the winter with him and his wife in Labrador City. Within a couple of weeks after Hedley's death, Beulah, along with her four youngest children—Dennis, Roxanne, Lisa, and Roger—packed their bags and headed north.

After living with Carson for a while, Beulah found a house of her own in Labrador City and moved in with the children.

For eleven-year-old Dennis Drover, the loss of his dad on Christmas Day and then suddenly being uprooted and separated from his Hodges Cove friends was extremely traumatic. At such an impressionable age, he wasn't sure how to deal with it all. For years he compartmentalized his fears, his sadness, and confusion by locking them away and kept everything inside. While it might have seemed to others that Dennis had moved on psychologically, he knew that, in fact, he had not even come close to finding closure. He might have stopped talking about the accident, but he certainly hadn't stopped thinking about it. That's why, in 2006, in conversation with Willis Thomas's brother Doug, Dennis mentioned an idea that he'd been carrying in his mind for years. He suggested establishing a memorial at the site where his dad and Willis died. Doug instantly knew it was a great idea and both men shared their thoughts on what to do next.

"We both drew sketches of an anchor, without the other knowing what we had done," Dennis says. So, with the basic concept determined, Doug, an excellent welder and handyman, along with his cousin and good friend Ray Stringer, started working on a steel anchor monument while the Drover and Thomas family members discussed the wording that would be engraved on it.

In the summer of 2007, both families invited everyone in Hodges Cove and area to join them for the unveiling. Dozens of people came, and for Dennis Drover a sense of closure was finally starting to seep in.

He unlocked that secret compartment in his mind and began talking to everyone about his private suffering. After all those silent years, Dennis's emotions still overwhelm him, but now he wants to talk about the tragedy and he's grown to understand and accept that his overt expressions of emotions and tears are all part of the healing process.

Also part of Dennis Drover's healing is a touching story about a small BIC lighter. "The only gift I ever gave my father that I paid for with my own money was a green BIC lighter—it was a Father's Day gift when I was very young," Dennis explains.

As fate would have it, shortly before the monument unveiling, Dennis was walking along the beach of Mooring Cove one day very close to the spot where his dad's body was found. It was one of those solemn times when he was reflecting on everything that had transpired since Christmas 1976, and especially the events of the last few days preparing for the unveiling of a memorial. Although he was lost in deep contemplation, his quiet thoughts suddenly vanished when he saw something that brought tears to his eyes and goosebumps on his flesh. There, lying on the beach, was a green BIC lighter. Picking it up, Dennis knew that it was not likely to be the same lighter that he had given his dad on Father's Day more than thirty years

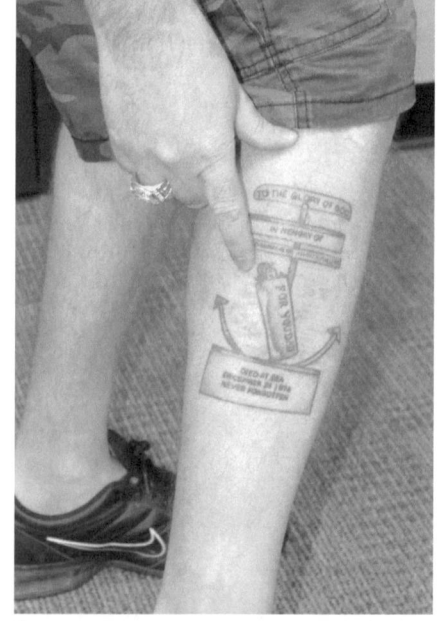

Dennis Drover shows the tattoo of a green BIC lighter, a symbol of the memory of his dad.

ago, but still, it seemed to Dennis that his father, Hedley, was there on the beach with him that day and was sending a sign from beyond the grave that he approved of what his son was doing. Dennis kept the little green lighter and, as an expression of how much that incident meant to him, Dennis now has a tattoo inked on his right leg with the image of the BIC along with the larger image of the anchor and monument.

The sudden loss of loved ones is never easy for families left behind, and undoubtedly there is an added dimension of sorrow when that loss occurs over Christmas. But the Thomases and Drovers of Hodges Cove have found a way to get by, and since the installation of the monument-memorial in 2007, both families have committed to coming home and gathering at the site every five years. The first reunion was in 2012 and plans are already under way for the next one in 2017.

Both families were drawn together in their common bond of sorrow, and the monument has become the focal point of sharing their memories and fostering even stronger family ties.

Monument erected in memory of Hedley Drover and Willis Thomas at the site of the accident

CHAPTER 10

Ronnie from River John

Is Ronnie Heighton a fisherman who is also a volunteer or is Ronnie Heighton a volunteer who happens to be a fisherman?

Well, unlike the popular television commercial, this is not a trick question. Ronnie is both, but his volunteerism occupies more time than his fishing these days.

The veteran fisherman is from River John, Nova Scotia, a picturesque little town on the Sunrise Trail overlooking the Northumberland Strait about twenty miles west of Pictou.

Ronnie is well-known to just about everyone in the fishing industry in Atlantic Canada. As vice-president of the Canadian Council of Professional Fish Harvesters, he is a regular fixture in the Association's booth at trade shows everywhere. He attends nearly all fisheries conferences in Atlantic Canada as well as others across the country. You can count on Ronnie to make his views known on just about any debate concerning fisheries matters. He is passionate about the industry and is always willing to share his opinion but is not belligerent. He takes the high road and is always respectful of the opinion of others.

I usually chat with Ronnie at fisheries trade shows in the Maritimes, and I was delighted to learn that he was inducted into Navigator/ Master Promotions' Atlantic Canada Marine Industries Hall of Fame at the Eastern Canadian Fisheries Expo in Yarmouth, Nova Scotia, in February 2013. It was there that I managed to sit down with Ronnie for a chat just minutes before his induction.

Ronnie collected his first old-age security cheque last year, but he says retirement is not on his horizon in the foreseeable future—either from fishing or from his volunteer responsibilities.

"I don't have any hobbies as such and I don't golf because golfers take the game far too seriously for my liking," he laughs.

When we talked about years gone by, Ronnie says everything is different now. On the fishing side of his life, he says he and most fellow fishermen in Northumberland Strait were "groundfish dependent," but with the collapse of the cod fishery in the early 1990s, they were forced to switch to scallop, herring, and lobster as their principal species. Earnings have not kept pace with rising expenses in running an enterprise and, like everyone else, Ronnie had to fish harder, longer, and with more gear to make a living until government restrictions and decreasing quotas made it almost impossible to make a decent living.

Things are more difficult in his volunteer activities, too. Besides being VP with the Canadian Professional Fish Harvesters, Ronnie is the longest-serving president of the Northumberland Fishermen's Association. He is a board member of the Eastern Fishermen's Federation (EFF), a board member of the Nova Scotia Fisheries Sector Council, and also a board member with his local Harbour Authority. For a little variety, he's also served on the heritage and museum committees in his region.

Ronnie Heighton accepts his Atlantic Canada Hall of Fame Mariner Award from Trevor Decker, a TriNav and *Navigator* Director.

"I like working with people, I like meeting new people, and for some reason, if something is not moving, or moving too slowly, I seem to get drawn to it and try to get it moving again," he says.

Ronnie says he has been privileged to have travelled and met interesting people as part of his volunteer work.

"I will never forget some of them. For example, I was in BC at a conference and this man who was Grand Chief of the First Nations groups in the region—he was eighty-six at the time but he had jet-black hair and looked years younger than his age—he spoke at the conference and for two solid hours had everyone's full attention. He was the most entertaining and informative speaker I have ever heard. No one in the audience wanted him to stop. His wisdom was amazing."

Obviously, a lot of his work with fisheries-related organizations means that Ronnie has to deal with government bureaucracies at all levels.

"And that's where the big change has been in recent years," he says.

Ronnie explains how, years ago, he could arrange a meeting with a middle-management person with the provincial government, and, at the end of the conversation, they had reached a firm decision on a course of action to follow and that would be it. Today, he says, bureaucrats can't make decisions. Everything gets passed on to another office, another level, until it reaches the federal level, and even then there is no solution. Fisheries and Oceans Canada (DFO) in Ottawa doesn't seem to want to make decisions anymore, he says.

"Almost everything is passed on to the Prime Minister's Office, and of course that's where it turns political and goes all out of whack," Ronnie states, adding that the bureaucracy constantly behaves as if the Prime Minister is going to call an election the next day, and so everything stagnates on the back burner.

"And of course all the cutbacks don't help, either," he says. "It looks to me that top managers don't want to cut people, opting instead to cut programs—and that makes it very hard to get things done, and it's very frustrating at times for people like us."

Ronnie smiles when he talks about River John. He was born there sixty-six years ago and his roots are deep.

"It was a wonderful place to grow up—there was never any crime and it's still more or less the same that way today," he says.

Unlike many rural communities, River John still has the same population as it had years ago, but Ronnie isn't sure how much longer that will last.

"We have a few new people coming to live there each year. Some are retiring from jobs in Ontario or out west and coming back home to enjoy their retirement, and we also have a few people settling there who just want a simpler lifestyle."

However, the fishing industry is no longer the employer that it once was, and it's getting hard to find people to work in fish plants anymore. Some plants even have to bring in workers from foreign countries.

"A plant in our area has a workforce of people from Thailand, and I'm afraid that pretty soon it's going to be the same in boats," Ronnie explains.

He doesn't blame young people for leaving when they can only expect a few weeks' work a year.

"Our lobster fishery is only about nine weeks and herring is less, about three or four weeks' work, and changes in the EI system are not adequate anymore [for survival], so our young people are going west where the jobs are year-round and the money is good, so I can see the day when we might have to hire foreign labour for our boats, too."

People who give of themselves through volunteering and spend countless days and weeks away from home struggling to help their industries are also getting harder to find. In fact, I caught up with Ronnie for our interview while he was on the road, and when I called him with a question just before going to print, he was in an airport on the way to a conference in Montreal. We all should be thankful for dedicated people like Ronnie Heighton.

CHAPTER 11

Lady Luck Elusive for Springdale Skipper

It's impossible to label Bon Pelley in a word or two. "Boat designer" comes to mind; businessman, too. There's also mechanic, fishing skipper, entrepreneur, and raconteur.

Possessing a life story worthy of a book, Bon is probably best known as the designer and builder of the largest fishing catamaran to fish commercially in Newfoundland and Labrador.

Bon grew up in Wild Bight (now Beachside). He moved to Toronto in his late teens and worked as an autobody mechanic.

He lived in the big city about six years or, as Bon puts it, "until I could save enough money to get out of it."

Back home in Beachside, he started his own body shop. Bon says he hardly made enough money for a coffee, and though he liked having his own business, he was happy when a new opportunity came along.

The Pentecostal Church minister asked if he'd be interested in providing a school bus service to transport students to and from school in Springdale. It sounded like a good idea, so he bought a bus and things went fairly well for a couple of years.

Then the church decided to put the bus service on tender. Bon was very surprised that someone he figured wasn't even eligible to bid got the contract. He thinks he lost the contract because he would often pick up Beachside kids from a different school or church than were also going to school in Springdale.

Bon Pelley relaxing at home in Springdale

"Sometimes they'd be out on the road in a snowstorm hitchhiking home and I thought it [giving them a ride] was the decent thing to do, so I'd stop and pick them up."

Bon's brother Melvin was a fisherman and, seemingly, doing well in the industry. Sometimes Melvin would drop by Bon's body shop and poke a bit of fun at his brother.

"He'd say that he was finished work for the day and I'd still be slaving away all hours of the day and night, six days a week," Bon says.

Bon mulled over the fishing concept and decided to give it a go. Never one to follow the customary path, Bon heard about a "boat with a difference" that was for sale. It was a former PT boat used at the US Navy station in Stephenville. PT boats were built of fine mahogany and oak wood and designed for high speed. It seemed like an unlikely fishing vessel, but Bon bought it anyway and prepared for his first fishing voyage: a sealing trip. Just after leaving port they ran into ice, but not enough to force them back to port. The inexperienced skipper was not fully aware of the serious damage that even thin ice can do to a vessel, and it wasn't long before the former PT boat was taking on water at the bow.

Fortunately, Melvin and his crew were nearby, but by the time Melvin got a line on the stem of his brother's boat, it was too late. When Melvin tried towing Bon's boat, she dug in deeper and kept on going down. Fortunately, Bon and the crew made it safely on board Melvin's boat.

Bon laughs today at his introduction to the fishing industry, also noting a sidebar story to the incident. He says several mean-spirited people circulated rumours that he deliberately sank his boat to collect insurance. However, the insurance paperwork had not been completed and he got nothing, a fact that he was painfully aware of as he watched his boat slip beneath the seas.

Bon tried his luck again and bought a boat in Fogo—one designed as a fishing vessel. Even this one got off to an ominous start.

"We went to Fogo to get her that winter, but she was frozen solid in about two feet of ice. We had to blast her out with dynamite," he laughs.

Bon fished cod for a while, but it was a tough business with small returns, so he tried something else. In the 1980s, he took a job as skipper on a Fishery Products International steel trawler and fished crab off northern Newfoundland. Crab sold for a mere twelve cents a pound in those days, but it was plentiful.

"We'd haul up a pot and the steel frames would bend under the strain," he says.

Bon Pelley is a natural storyteller: a raconteur. He delights in spinning endless and detailed yarns about his life's journey, melding the fun times with his troubled days. Now in his seventies and retired, he laughs at them all, especially the ones that weren't funny at the time.

He's one of thousands of fishermen who have been frustrated to no end by government bureaucracies and senseless policies that cost him hundreds of thousands of dollars. He talks of guidelines crafted in St. John's and Ottawa by people who knew nothing about life on board a fishing vessel. He talks about skulduggery in the industry and he talks about bureaucrats strictly enforcing laws for some and turning a blind eye for others.

Even carrying out a good deed cost him dearly.

A boat close to Bon broke down while crab fishing far offshore and Bon was asked by government authorities to tow the disabled vessel to port. By the time he got back to the fishing grounds, the Department of Fisheries and Oceans Canada (DFO) had closed the fishery, so he missed the last several days of lucrative fishing that season.

Besides the initial loss of income, the biggest cost of that deed came later. His future quotas would be forever small because they were based on his current season's landings—a small catch that year meant a small quota in future.

"It cost me thousands and thousands of dollars." It seems that being a good Samaritan doesn't pay for Bon.

Of all Bon's endeavours, the design and construction of a large wave-piercing catamaran in Springdale would be his boldest. The three-year project was done in conjunction with various government agencies, and whether the venture was a success or not depends largely on what you consider to be the fundamental purpose for the project. Capable of travelling at nearly double the speed of traditional vessels and using the same amount of fuel seemed to make sense to Bon.

Safety was also a consideration, due to a close call he experienced personally. He and his son Paul got caught out in a vicious storm off northern Newfoundland on a crab fishing trip several years prior to building the innovative twin hull. Bon says when they heard the forecast they knew there wasn't time enough to steam the 150 miles to port. They could have made it if they'd had a faster vessel, and that was when he started thinking about a catamaran.

The catamaran *Atlanticat*

The cat cost a lot more than projected, but Bon thinks it might have worked better had they been allowed to build it twenty feet longer. Government fisheries regulations forced him to build the vessel less than sixty-five feet—too short to be totally functional. The *Atlanticat* later wound up working for the Marine Institute in St. John's as a research vessel.

Bon's last business heartache came in 2006 when the *Sealer*, his wooden-hull vessel, burnt at the wharf in Springdale, just a few feet from where the *Atlanticat* was docked. The blaze also destroyed expensive fishing gear that was stowed on the wharf nearby. The *Sealer* was beyond repair and insurance covered about two-thirds of his loss. The nets and seines were not insured.

But Bon Pelley also had a lot of success.

Today, he and his wife live in obvious comfort in a very nice home in Springdale, with several other expensive possessions, including a large motor home parked in his driveway when I was there. The fact that he had been just a stroke of bad luck away from so many potentially successful ventures that could have meant significant wealth for him now provides great fodder for his storytelling. His successful ventures don't make for as many laughs.

Bon is a pleasant and jovial man who laughs heartily at his own folly. His memoir would be a most compelling read.

CHAPTER 12

Season of Small Mackerel

In southwest Nova Scotia, a fishing season that produced catches of mainly small mackerel used to be considered a harbinger of bad luck or a bad omen—a sign that something bad was going to happen before the season was over. Well, in July 1957, the mackerel run produced mainly small fish, and for the fishing village of Sluice Point, near Yarmouth, something awful did happen.

Paul LeBlanc was a happy fifteen-year-old that year.

"He loved everything and anything to do with the outdoors. He was always smiling and laughing," recalls his good friend and school classmate at the time Alain Meuse (the same Alain Meuse who has contributed to the *Navigator* magazine).

Alain says he doesn't recall Paul saying what he wanted to be when he finished school, but Alain said it would have to be something that involved working outdoors because his young friend was an outdoors natural. Paul's sister agrees.

"He probably would have been a fisherman, because he was in a boat every chance he got," says Anne Marie (LeBlanc) Surette, who is one year older than her brother Paul.

July 18, 1957, was a nice summer's day in Sluice Point, located about a ten-minute drive from Yarmouth. Paul's uncle Zachary "Cario" Surette was owner of a Cape Island–style lobster boat, and on Wednesday, July 17, he had mentioned to some friends that he was going digging for Irish moss the next day, but first he would likely try and catch some mackerel.

Small mackerel was especially good lobster bait, and with the good summer run of young mackerel, it would be an opportunity to stock up on bait for the lobster fishery later in the fall.

Sluice Point is a small community of approximately 200 people, and everyone was like extended family. When word got out that Zachary was going mackerel fishing the next day, several young teenagers asked if they could join him, because mackerel, especially the small ones, were fun to catch. One of those looking for a fun day was young Paul LeBlanc. Joanne (Bourque) Moulaison was another.

Joanne remembers that they were waiting for Paul to arrive on Thursday morning. Zachary didn't want to leave without his nephew, so they waited a few minutes longer when finally they saw Paul running toward the wharf as fast as he could. Joanne says there were several people on board the Cape Islander, so Paul decided to get in the small skiff that was tied to the stern of the larger boat to be towed to the fishing grounds just offshore.

Memories of precise details of what happened next on that Thursday morning have faded—after all, it was nearly sixty years ago—but one thing they know is that when the fishing vessel steamed under the Sluice Point bridge, the bow of the small boat was pulled down and sea water came flooding into the skiff.

Southwest Nova Scotia is known for extreme tides that run almost as high or low and as fast as tides in nearby Bay of Fundy. Alain says that, at high tide, motoring underneath the bridge was relatively comfortable, but at mid-tide the current was very fast, making it difficult to manoeuvre a vessel, especially boats with small power. With a fast running current, it is likely that the skiff was behaving with a jerking or zigzagging motion that would cause the tow line to slacken and tighten involuntarily and ultimately might cause the towed boat to submerge its stem. Whatever the case, fifteen-year-old Paul LeBlanc was thrown overboard in a heavy current that would have been difficult even for a strong swimmer to navigate, but Paul couldn't swim at all and most likely panicked.

Joanne says she saw Paul fall overboard, but like most other people who witness a tragedy unfolding at a young age, she doesn't recall any other details of what happened next. She says she never could remember much other than seeing Paul falling from the skiff and disappearing beneath the water with his arms raised above his head.

Zachary turned the big boat around as quickly as he could, but with the strong current impeding his ability to control the boat, by the time he eventually returned to where Paul had fallen, there was no sign of his nephew.

The same current that gave Zachary trouble turning around

also meant that, in a few short minutes, it would be impossible to know where to search for Paul; he would have been pushed rapidly along with the current. After circling the area several times, Zachary went back to port and notified the authorities and, along with other boats, returned to search for the missing teenager. But it was in vain.

Alain remembers grieving for his friend in the days following Paul's drowning.

"The nights were especially hard," he says. "I recall looking out over the ocean at the islands in the area and thinking that he's out there somewhere and he needs to be found."

Even as a teenager, Alain seemed to understand that families needed to see the body of a lost loved one. Otherwise, finding closure is very difficult, if not impossible. When Alain became a fisheries reporter in later years, he would have that belief confirmed many times.

"I remember one night about a week or so after Paul fell overboard—it was almost a full moon and I kept thinking that his body should be coming ashore sometime soon because there was an incoming tide," he says.

Sure enough, on July 28, ten days after the accident, searchers found Paul's body washed up on the shoreline of one of the outlying islands near Sluice Point.

Three days later, Alain experienced one of his most unpleasant tasks. He was a pallbearer for his classmate and good friend Paul LeBlanc, who had made his final voyage at the tender age of fifteen.

It was indeed a tragic "season of small mackerel" for a close-knit community in southwest Nova Scotia, where every family was touched by sorrow with the loss of a vibrant young person who had what seemed to be a bright future ahead, but who was suddenly was snatched away.

CHAPTER 13

I Died Once and That's Enough

Lesley Peddle admits that she is a little different than most women. Now in her thirties, Lesley has owned motorcycles since she was sixteen. She currently owns a Harley Davidson. She is a scuba diver and also owns a bright orange Chevy 4 x 4 truck. Lesley is mate on a sixty-five-foot steel crab vessel out of St. John's, Newfoundland, but she has also captained vessels as well. And she loves to cook.

Lesley's parents are Newfoundlanders, but her dad was a military man, so they lived in several regions. However, the place she calls home is Oromocto, New Brunswick, because that's where she spent her most memorable years.

After high school, Lesley was intent on following a career in veterinary medicine.

An owner of two purebred dogs, Lesley's love of animals is as strong as her zest for life. But then, in her late teens, Lesley developed a relationship with a man in the fishing industry and decided that she'd take a look at that line of work. The thought of being the only woman working on a fishing vessel with a bunch of men was daunting, especially for an eighteen-year-old landlubber.

Her first boat was a sixty-one-foot vessel that was not equipped with many of today's technologies or creature comforts.

"There was no shelter on deck and you could barely stand up in the hold," Lesley remembers.

Lesley on her Harley
(Photo courtesy of Lesley Peddle)

But none of that mattered much on her first fishing trip.

"I didn't get out of the bunk for five days. Seasick," she says.

However, despite a less than auspicious start to a new career, she persisted in the stubborn and determined style of her military upbringing and stuck with it. Lesley eventually took on more and more responsibility and became a mate. It was then that her comfort level in the business increased and the seasickness disappeared.

Along with her survival instinct, Lesley went to school and studied her craft. She now holds a Master Class III certificate and has nearly completed all requirements for her Class II. Lesley is now qualified as an oceangoing master of a fishing vessel.

Lesley battled seasickness for a couple of years, but the sickest time of her life happened in 2009 when she was a victim of an R2 refrigerant gas leak in the hold of the vessel *Rebel's Pride*.

On watch in the wheelhouse, Lesley noticed two crew members on deck near the fish hold behaving erratically. Sensing that something was seriously wrong, she pulled the engine out of gear and ran to the deck to investigate. She saw that not only were the two deckhands affected by something odd, she saw the vessel's skipper, Chris Peddle, sprawled at the bottom of the hold. Lesley climbed down the ladder into the hold, and within a few seconds, as she was trying to drag Chris on deck, Lesley suddenly went as limp as a rag doll and passed out. Due to the quick thinking and action of shipmate Lisa Heffern, along with the help of one of the deckhands, Chris and Lesley were eventually brought back to life, but for a while it appeared that Lesley was dead.

Lesley's close brush with death was a life-altering experience.

"I died once and that's enough for now," she laughs, adding that the experience changed the way she approaches life on a daily basis now.

Lesley started to pay more attention to safety practices, especially at sea. She's taken all the safety courses available to prepare for any possible accidents. Not only does she caution others to make sure their vessels are equipped with life-saving

Lesley (third from left) and crew of *Newfoundland Explorer*
(Photo courtesy of Lesley Peddle)

technology, she insists that her new crew members are also trained to respond appropriately if anything happens to her again.

"It's fine for me to know what to do, but I need them to know in case something happens to me, too," she explains.

Lesley's scuba diving expertise came in handy in the Davis Strait off Greenland once. She was captain of a turbot vessel when word came in that a nearby ship, the *Nain Banker*, had rope tangled around its propeller. Leslie donned her diving gear and successfully cut the ropes and freed the prop, allowing the vessel to resume operations. Lesley's help saved the company a lot of money because it allowed the vessel to go back to work in just a matter of a few hours. Otherwise, the *Nain Banker* might have required towing to port to effect repairs.

Besides battling a tendency toward seasickness, Lesley had other negatives to contend with in her early days at sea.

Not all of her shipmates liked the idea of having a woman on board and made no bones about letting their feelings known. It wasn't the old superstition that a woman on a boat would bring bad luck. It seemed they thought a woman wouldn't be able to do what they considered a "man's job."

She smiles when she recalls incidents when doubters watch her every move wondering how capable she was. She remembers more than one occasion while crab fishing when she was under close scrutiny.

When the heavy crab traps started coming out of water, Lesley grabbed the first pot and carried it to the deck with the ease of any man.

"They're there lookin' at me with the jaw just hanging open," she says.

Some of her shipmates who didn't want a woman on board at first are now some of her best friends.

"Some of the guys are fine, but some just seem to want to try and twist your mind," she says.

Lesley earned the respect of one or two shipmates once during a seal-hunting trip.

"We were sealing, I was the gunner on board the boat—up in the bow—and one of the boys had trouble getting from the ice and back on the boat. I managed to get him alongside [the boat] and grabbed him by the back of his pants and flipped him in over the gunwales," she explains in a matter-of-fact tone of voice.

The body weight of a bulky fisherman, combined with several pounds of heavy boots and clothing, is not easy to haul up the side of a boat to safety. It is my guess that, besides being relieved to be safe on board the boat, that sealer was impressed with his rescuer.

"I think the guys realize that I'm not out there to make their coffee," Lesley says with a grin.

When Lesley is not riding her Harley, cruising in her truck, scuba diving, fishing, or cooking, you might find her at her artwork. She likes to draw landscapes, fish, and animals. She wishes she had more time to pursue her artistic passion, but even a person who approaches life with the energy of a volcano has to draw the line somewhere and recognize that there are only twenty-four hours in a day.

Lesley truly enjoys her job, and though it's not on the front burner all

Fun in Northumberland Strait; Confederation Bridge to PEI in background. (Photo courtesy of Lesley Peddle)

the time, she has given thought to owning her own vessel and enterprise one day. She is also actively involved in building her own dog-breeding kennel business. Lesley Peddle has lived more life in the six year's since her near-death experience in 2009 than most people do in sixty years. And I think she's only just begun.

CHAPTER 14

Beware a Greasy Sky

No matter what career they choose, most Newfoundland and Labrador men are avid wildlife and outdoor enthusiasts. They long for a day in the woods moose hunting, rabbit catching, or for a day on the water fishing or saltwater bird hunting. That lifestyle has always been part of the province's culture and continues to be just as strong today as ever.

In December 1965, Don Reid was branch manager of the Bank of Nova Scotia in Lewisporte, on Newfoundland's northeast coast. His friend and colleague Ken George was assistant manager and loans officer at the same branch.

On Saturday morning, December 11, 1965, both men were up before dawn and wondering how they would spend their day off. Both observed that the weather was more like a day in August than a couple of weeks before Christmas. The temperature was about twelve degrees Celcius and there was not even a hint of a breeze.

What a great day on the water, they thought.

Ken, owner of a twenty-one-foot motorboat, phoned Don and suggested they go turr (murre) hunting. It didn't take much arm twisting to get Don on side, but they both agreed that because Notre Dame Bay was full of small islands, it would be wise to have a fisherman or someone who knew the bay intimately to accompany them. After all, regardless of the nice beginning to the day, the northeast coast of Newfoundland is an area that can produce rapid change in weather, especially in December.

Frank Greenham in his home carpentry shop

They both thought their friend Frank Greenham from Newstead–Comfort Cove would be the ideal person to join them. Ken's boat was docked in Cottles Island and Frank was located along the way to the island from Lewisporte.

"I wasn't fussy about going when Don called," Frank remembers.

Among other things, Frank owned and operated a small garage and service station at the junction of what is now called the Road to the Isles and the branch road to Comfort Cove.

"Saturday was always our busiest day of the week, but it was more than that. There was something making me feel uneasy, like an inner voice saying I shouldn't go out in boat that day," Frank recalls.

One of Frank Greenham's hobbies is model boat building

"Come on, Frank, take a break, you deserve it," Don said, laughing, knowing that Frank worked hard and a turr hunting trip would probably be good for him. Frank turned to his wife and asked if she could take care of the business for a couple of hours if he decided to go with his friends. She agreed, but Frank says that she, too, felt a strong and strange sense of uneasiness.

"Meanwhile, I was concerned about saying no to these fellows, because even though they were good friends, they were also my bankers and I wanted to stay on their good side, 'cause you never know when you might need their help," Frank says, smiling.

So, despite being busy and feeling a little edgy, Frank agreed to join his banker friends. Because the plan was to be back home by lunchtime, Frank didn't bother dressing in clothing that he would ordinarily wear on a boating trip in December, and he didn't bother taking any warm clothes with him. He left his rubber boots, coat, and mitts at home. He didn't even bother to bring a lunch. The only thing he took was his twelve-gauge shotgun.

When Ken and Don arrived at the service station to pick him up, Frank jumped in the truck dressed as he would for working at the station on a warm day. Perhaps it was partly due to the way he was dressed, but Frank immediately noted that both Ken and Don were wearing rubber boots and warm clothes, appropriate for surviving a winter storm.

"Glad you could come, Frank," said Don. "We'll get a good meal of turrs today for sure. I hear there are lots of them just out the bay. I have a drop of black rum, too, so we can have a little nip on the way."

Frank facetiously replied that he didn't like rum, but it might come in handy.

About 9:00 a.m., the putt-putt sound of Ken's make and break four-horsepower Acadia engine echoed off the cliffs on a perfectly calm morning. Frank soon forgot about his previous nagging concerns as he sat in the front of the small boat and enjoyed the spectacular scenery of sunny Notre Dame Bay and the reflections on the calm ocean from several of the dozens of islands that dot the bay's coastline. It was indeed a great day on the water.

"How far out the bay did you say the turrs were?" Frank asked Don.

"About eight or nine miles out from Western Head," Don replied.

Frank suddenly realized that they were not going to be back by lunchtime—not in a boat that only steams about five miles an hour. Steam time alone would be at least four hours, and that didn't include hunting time.

"How much gas do you have, Ken?" Frank called to his buddy at the back of the boat with one hand on the tiller.

"I got a little bit there. Why?" Ken replied.

"Because we're still going out and we'll have a long way back in," Frank said.

Frank was about to follow up with another question, but that's when Don sang out that he saw a turr. Ken slowed the engine and, within a couple of minutes, the first turr of the day was in the boat. Shortly afterwards, there were another two birds on board and more sighted a few yards away.

Things were going just great, and Don's promise of getting a lot of turrs looked very likely. But in all the excitement, Frank noticed that the sky was no longer blue.

"I noticed that the sky was already very dark to the southeast and it was moving our way," Frank says.

Keeping an eye on the changing weather, Frank thought he should alert his friends. "Boys, there's a greasy-looking sky to the southeast. I don't like the look of it at all. I think there's snow in it and I think we should head for land."

Don and Ken agreed that the sky did indeed look "greasy" and realized that it was about 1:00 p.m. and darkness would soon be closing in, especially if it became overcast and started to snow. They also realized that they were about two hours away from land. Their concerns heightened when they noticed there were no other boats in the area in case they needed help.

As Ken started the little four-horsepower Acadia engine, the wind suddenly breezed up and the ocean was no longer calm.

"It was no time before there were whitecaps on the water and the temperature started to drop," Frank says.

What was supposed to be a fun three- or four-hour turr hunting trip became the longest nightmare in the lives of three men.

Glancing at the dark, menacing sky to the southeast, Frank knew that there was snow coming soon, possibly within an hour. As the waves starting foaming into whitecaps, and with the temperature dropping, the experienced seaman worried they would wind up in a snowstorm and lose sight of land.

Being caught offshore in a December storm in Ken's small open boat in Notre Dame Bay, Newfoundland, was a scary thought. It was then that Frank remembered he was dressed only in street clothes, without even a jacket, warm boots, or gloves to wear.

"Ken, get out your compass. I think we should take a bearing for Black Island because it's the closest point of land and there are people living on the island," Frank said, explaining to his friend that they might need to get ashore soon.

Ken looked through a couple of boxes on board his little boat and soon realized that he had left his compass home on the kitchen table.

"I remember saying to myself, 'My God, this is not looking good,'" Frank recalls.

Having determined earlier that they were also low on gas, a compass was more essential now than ever in case they wound up adrift.

Don may have been silently sharing Frank's thoughts and decided that now was as good a time as any to pour a drink of the rum he had brought along.

"Here, boys. Have a little nip of this to keep your blood warm," he said, passing Ken and Frank small plastic containers filled with his favourite brew.

After assessing their options, Frank looked at Don, who was "on the tiller" steering the boat, and offered some advice.

"Keep the wind on her port bow—on the left side of your face, Don—that way we should stay headed toward the island."

Minutes later, the wind increased significantly, seas grew rougher, and snow started lashing against the men's faces as they peered straight into the brewing storm, hoping to get an occasional glimpse of land.

But their hopes were in vain. As it grew colder and winds increased, visibility was reduced from kilometres ahead to mere metres. Frank says he also remembers thinking that the wind had changed from the southeast to the northeast, although he couldn't be certain.

"With a southeast wind, temperatures don't normally get all that cold, and I can tell you, sir, it was getting colder by the minute," he recalls.

By 4:30 p.m., conditions had deteriorated. It was almost totally dark, the temperature had dropped to below freezing, and winds had whipped up to about forty miles per hour, creating high waves. But worst of all, it was now snowing heavily. In a nutshell, they were caught at sea in a small twenty-one-foot open boat in a full-blown northeast Newfoundland blizzard.

Shortly after dark, the winds and waves were so high that the boat wasn't making any headway at all. As the men huddled in conversation, they decided that keeping the engine running was merely wasting valuable fuel that they might need later. As Ken shut off the motor, Frank pointed out they needed to keep the bow headed into the wind, because now that they were drifting and at the mercy of nature, a strong gust of wind combined with a large wave hitting the side of the boat could easily capsize it. Frank noticed there was no anchor on board, so he filled a five-gallon bucket with water, lowered it a few feet below the surface, and tied the rope to the stem of the boat, to make what is known as a sea anchor. The weight of the bucket helped keep the little boat heading into the wind.

Now that the engine was shut off, the sounds of the howling winds and roaring seas seemed louder and more ferocious than before. With nothing more to do than sit and pray, the three men hardly spoke. Freezing spray was constantly blowing over them, and while Ken and Don were dressed appropriately, Frank, clad only in light clothing, was already soaked to the skin and losing body heat.

"I was shaking like a leaf on a tree, and that's when it first dawned on me that we could be out there all night, because there was no point in sending out a search party in that kind of storm," Frank recalls.

About midnight, the three bird hunters heard what they initially thought was a strange sound. At first, neither of them thought it was the sound of an engine or a vessel because it was more like a rumbling noise. As the sound grew closer and louder, Frank, who was a mechanical engineer, recognized the familiar rumblings of a large vessel rather than the small fishing boat or pleasure craft that they were expecting to hear. They didn't have any flares to fire, so they frantically shot off several rounds of gunshots in hopes that someone on the approaching ship would hear them.

But it was not to be. A couple of minutes later, the sound of the vessel that came close enough for them to feel its wake faded into the darkness.

Surprisingly, the men were more philosophical than dejected about losing the possibility of rescue.

"It could have been worse," one fellow said. "We could have been cut down and smashed to pieces and no one would have ever known."

Nodding in agreement, the other two were somehow buoyed by the fact that they were spared certain death, and now they seemed more determined to survive the storm. In their moment of appreciation, another fellow chimed in with a reminder that their small boat was handling the rough seas like a trooper.

"You know, that little boat rode the tops of those waves like a duck," Frank says. "It was almost like she was in someone's big hand that was keeping her afloat on top of those high breaking waves. I'll never understand it as long as I live."

Even though the boat was riding the seas very well indeed, spray from the cresting waves kept throwing water over the gunwales. Taking turns bailing out water, all three were in surprisingly good condition and said that if they could hang on till daylight, the storm might lose some of its fury and a rescue party would be along to bring them home.

Little did they know that there would be yet another night and two days of hell to go through before home would become a reality.

Surviving Saturday afternoon and night on board a small open boat in a December blizzard required tremendous determination and strong survival skills.

Don and Ken huddled on the floorboards in the midsection of the boat as Frank placed his cold wet feet between their bodies to stave off frostbite. As the boat drifted aimlessly in Notre Dame Bay, they hoped and prayed that they would see land soon. Their hopes of better weather conditions at daylight were dashed when, if anything, it seemed to get worse with strengthening winds and even colder temperatures.

Meanwhile, back home, Frank's brother Jack contacted the owner and captain of a large passenger boat to ask if he would consider searching for the overdue bird hunters. Captain Harvey Bulgin was an experienced mariner and didn't want to give Jack false hopes.

"Unless they reached land somewhere last night and got ashore, their chances of surviving this storm in a small boat like that are not very good," he said.

However, he obligingly left his home port of Summerford and searched for some time, but visibility was nil in the blizzard and his search turned up nothing. Turning to Jack, Captain Bulgin said he had never seen a storm any worse and it was simply too dangerous and futile to try going on. Jack understood and agreed.

Despite their faces, feet, and hands being numb from the bitter cold, the three men were still determined to fight the still-raging storm conditions on Sunday morning and make it through another day. Surely their drifting boat would have to strike land somewhere soon, they thought. Finally, Frank thought he saw a flashing light. Not sure if he should say anything at first, because he was aware that hallucinating is common when one becomes hypothermic, Frank remained quiet but looked more intently through the drifting snow. A few seconds later, he saw another flash.

"Boys, I think I see a light," Frank exclaimed. Don and Ken raised their heads and both confirmed that Frank was not hallucinating.

"Yes, yes it is, I can see it, too," they both said, daring to hope their ordeal might soon be over.

"I wonder if it's a lighthouse? Ken, see if the engine will start. Don, take the tiller, but be careful and keep away from the shore for a while until we size things up," Frank said, taking control of the situation.

"I couldn't believe it, but that little engine started on the first swing of the flywheel," Frank says, smiling.

As the small motorboat rode the waves, the three men kept scanning the shoreline for a suitable place to land. Rounding a headland, they could hear the distinct blast of a foghorn, but they still had no idea where they were. The water was slightly calmer than they had experienced for the past twenty-four hours.

"Let's try to land in there," Ken shouted, pointing to a small rocky cove. "We'll probably lose the boat because there's no beach, but we got to try to save ourselves." Frank and Don nodded in agreement as they prepared to jump as soon as the boat struck the rocks.

A minute later, they clambered from the little boat to safety as they grabbed their guns, gas can, paddles, turrs, and whatever they could save before the seas started battering the boat against the rocks. It was with heavy hearts as the three watched the seas pound the little boat that served them so incredibly well and brought them safely through a terrible blizzard. Before long, the boat was smashed to small pieces and strewn along the rocky shoreline.

Finding a place at the base of a high hill that was somewhat sheltered from the storm, the men managed to build a fire. They could still hear the foghorn but couldn't see the light. Their first priority was to try and warm their bodies and thaw their frozen clothes before attempting to walk though deep snow.

Although they were on land, the men were still far from safety. The only way to get a better idea of where they were was to climb the steep hill in waist-deep snow and hope to see the lighthouse beacon. It was a struggle, but they managed to climb to the top of the hill toting their guns and a couple of other provisions, but with daylight and heavy drifting they could not see the flashing light.

"Let's take a few minutes and catch our breath—and how about another sip of that black rum, eh?" Don said. Frank still believes the rum was helpful and is thankful to Don for bringing it, even if he wasn't fussy about the taste.

After a short rest, the men trudged on through the deep snow toward the sound of the foghorn. In retrospect, Frank thinks they might have been going around in circles, because the sound of the horn seemed to come from different directions at various times, when they were on top of a hill or down in a valley.

Finally, by late Sunday afternoon, the men were exhausted and hungry. They agreed to stop and light another fire and Ken and Don opened their sandwiches to share with Frank, who had left home without food. Frank decided to heat his sandwich over the fire but didn't realize it was sealed in saran wrap—it melted into his sandwich. After two days without food, Frank's hunger was too great to worry about trivial matters like eating plastic.

"It wasn't too bad at all," he jokes.

During their rest, Frank noticed his feet were bleeding. He removed his boot from one foot but couldn't get it back on because his feet had swollen and the flesh had been torn away. The rest of the journey would have to be made in stocking feet.

It was almost dark, and as badly as the men wanted to rest longer, they knew that time was running out. They had to find shelter soon. In the darkness of night they could once again see the flashing light in the distance and trudged steadily onward through the snow, too tired and numb to feel pain, even Frank with his shoeless feet. Finally, just after daylight on Monday morning, Frank climbed to the top of a small hill while Don and Ken waited to see if they were still going in the right direction.

"I wondered if I was dreaming, but just a short distance away I saw the lighthouse, and the lightkeeper was out on the platform," says Frank. "Thank God—we made it!" Shouting first to Ken and Don to come quickly, Frank then shouted to get the lightkeeper's attention.

"We practically slid down the hill on the ice and snow like we were on snowboards, we were so excited," he said.

Once in the warmth and comfort of the lightkeeper's residence, they learned they were on Exploits Island in Notre Dame Bay. The men were given dry clothes and fed warm food. The lightkeeper's wife treated Frank's seriously injured foot, and despite more than two days and nights of survival against unbelievably terrible conditions, all three were in relatively good condition by the end of the day on Monday.

They had been given up for dead by many, but Frank Greenham, Ken George, and Don Reid beat the odds. On Tuesday, December 14, 1965, they were reunited with their families back home in Lewisporte and Newstead–Comfort Cove.

Their final voyage would have to wait for another day.

CHAPTER 15

Working to Make Things Better

"I've gone from being Scottish to Irish." That's how Lisa Fitzgerald responds when asked about her name change in 2012.

Lisa has been known to almost everyone in the Nova Scotia fishing industry for many years as Lisa Anderson. Lisa laughs and jokes that when people ask her about the name change, because at forty-something, she says, they assume she got divorced. In fact, Lisa got married last year.

However, knowing that the name change will take time to evolve for many of her clients and acquaintances, Lisa has kept her old email address—the one that has "Anderson" in it.

Lisa is the executive director of the Nova Scotia Fisheries Sector Council based in Yarmouth in southwest Nova Scotia. She's held that position since the Council was formed, although she was actually connected even before the organization was established. She explains that the Sector Council grew out of the old Regional Industries Training Commission (RITC).

Lisa Anderson-Fitzgerald

Lisa graduated with a business degree from Mount St. Vincent's University in the 1990s and joined the RITC in 1996. A few years later, the government decided to focus less on training and, through structural changes in funding, a new body that was focused more on human resource development was formed.

The idea was to be more project-oriented, so the old RITC was transformed into a sector council. In southwest Nova Scotia, the fishing industry was high on the list of prominent industry sectors, and the Nova Scotia Fisheries Sector Council office was set up in Yarmouth.

Lisa Anderson-Fitzgerald was born and bred in Yarmouth. She says her grandparents had a restaurant located just a couple of minutes' walk from where the council office is now located.

"I used to ride my bicycle there all the time," she says, pointing out her office window at a field across the street where that restaurant was situated.

"I was lucky to get a job back home when I finished university," she says.

Lisa says Yarmouth was a nice place to grow up. Big enough to offer good schools and facilities, it was also small enough to have that homey environment that is lacking in large cities.

"It was a busier place when I was a kid than it is today—tourism was bigger and there were more motels and hotels than now," she says, noting that Yarmouth has suffered financially since the US (Bar Harbor–Yarmouth) ferry ceased operations a few years ago.

Lisa is all about fisheries these days, even though she's not from a fishing family, although she has plenty of marine connections. Her father was a marine engineer. Her grandfather and great-grandfather were all marine people who worked on ferry boats.

Sadly, her father was killed in an accident on board the Yarmouth–Bar Harbor ferry ship *Bluenose* in 1991.

Lisa was just twenty-one and in her third year of university at the time. She remembers the tragedy as a life-changing event for her. Safety is a very close-to-the-heart matter for Lisa today in her involvement with fishermen who work in the most dangerous occupation in the world.

"I don't publicly go out and say that I've been touched personally by tragedy or whatever, but we're all about prevention and I think it's probably giving back, in some way, in that I don't ever want to see anyone having to go through what I did, and I suspect there is some kind of inner push to do that because of my personal experience."

Her first boss in the former Industries Training Commission was Denny Morrow. If that name rings a bell, it's because he was one of the best-known people in the entire Nova Scotia fishing industry, having served for many years as director of the Nova Scotia Fish Packers Association.

Lisa says having access to Denny's vast wealth of fisheries knowledge was a tremendous asset. Denny's office was literally next door, across the hall from Lisa's office on John Street in Yarmouth. Denny has retired, but he still stops by for a chat now and then.

Lisa says she enjoys working with fishing people. She says fishermen are among the most direct communicators anywhere and are not shy about expressing their feelings on any issue. She says she learned an important lesson in dealing with fishermen a long time ago.

"I discovered that it's a lot easier to find out what fishermen don't want than it is to learn what they do want."

Like their counterparts in Newfoundland and Labrador and the rest of Atlantic Canada, fishermen are quick to tell you in no uncertain terms when they think an idea won't work or why a government policy was ill-conceived.

"So, I discovered that working with fishermen on the negative side first makes it easier to get to why a different approach may be a better option. I say, 'Okay, well, now that we know what you don't want, can we explore ways to find something that will work for you?'"

In her quest to find what works for them, Lisa has earned a lot of respect from fishermen. She's comfortable at the head table facilitating forums and meetings on a variety of issues. Seldom rattled when tempers get hot, she has a way of calming the room, keeping the meeting on an even keel, and staying with the agenda.

Having said that, Lisa chuckles when asked about what projects she's working on these days.

"Well, professionalization is still on the table," she says, laughing, because trying to develop a registration and professionalization program for Nova Scotia fishermen has been an ongoing effort for many years that has often been frustrating for Lisa.

She jokes that when she's looking back over the years while giving her retirement speech decades from now, she will still be talking about professionalization.

"I'll be saying, 'Well, we almost got professionalization. We're still working on it, but we're almost there.'"

Jokes aside, professionalization and certification are taking a long time, with progress moving at a snail's pace. Nova Scotia fishermen are not convinced that there is any benefit in the concept and they are wary of it.

However, legislation was passed in the Nova Scotia legislature last year to open the way for registration and certification of fishermen similar to legislation that has been in effect in Newfoundland and Labrador for many years.

On a personal note, Lisa and her husband enjoy outdoor activities.

"Running is my biggest hobby. I ran a half-marathon—twenty-one kilometres—last year. It was the farthest I'd ever run at one time," she said. "Other than running, we enjoy camping and outdoor activities. My husband has a motorcycle and I enjoy that as well."

CHAPTER 16

From Make and Breaks to Engines as Big as Houses

Do you have a question about make and break engines? You need to know Max Clarke.

Max grew up in Labrador in the 1950s and early 1960s in the era when the make and break was the king of engines in Newfoundland and Labrador. After a distinguished career as a marine engineer working on marine engines of almost every description on board vessels of all shapes and sizes, Max still has an Acadian make and break engine in his shed in Paradise, near St. John's. He's owned several, including one that he donated to a Newfoundland museum.

Visiting with Max in his modest bungalow just a couple minutes' drive from St. John's, you are regaled with fascinating stories about the various kinds of make and breaks and their significant role in the history and culture of Newfoundland and Labrador, especially in the fishing industry.

He says the most common names of make and break engines in this province included Atlantic, Acadian, Hubbard, and Myannis. Other brands included Palmer, Bridgeport, and Imperial, and, according to Max, the E. F. Barnes Company in St. John's made a make and break engine they simply called "The Barnes" that became popular in the 1950s.

And then there's the Coaker. Some people argue that there was

Max Clarke looks through some of the many documents he had kept of his travels.

no Coaker make and break engine as such. However, William Coaker, founder of the Fishermen's Protective Union (FPU), ordered a large number of engines from an established manufacturing company to distribute to union members (fishermen), and because the order was so significant, the company honoured Coaker by naming those engines after him. However, there is another argument that claims Coaker demanded changes or modifications to the company's standard make and break engine. They say the company agreed to the union leader's request, thereby making the Coaker a unique engine.

Max says the make and break was built so simply that foundries and engine companies just about everywhere were making them. In some cases the make and break gave a solid start to companies that grew to become some of the most prominent in the engine business to this day.

Batteau, Labrador, childhood home of Max

But there is much more to Max Clarke than his knowledge of make and break engines. He is also passionate about his Labrador heritage. An orphan, Max spent winters inland in Porcupine Bay and summers in Batteau, on the southern Labrador Coast. He went to elementary school in Cartwright and attended high school in St. Anthony on the island.

Chat for a few minutes with Max and you will soon realize that one of his pet peeves is how few people in Newfoundland know anything about Batteau and its significance to coastal Labrador.

"They don't even know where it is," he says emphatically. "When Karl Wells was weatherman on CBC TV, every night for twenty years or so he would give the forecast 'from Batteau to L'Anse au Clair,' and yet people say they've never heard of Batteau. Unbelievable!"

It's easy to understand why Max is perturbed by that ignorance.

Batteau was one of the best fishing areas in the province, not to mention a great harbour where hundreds of (island) Newfoundland fishing crews congregated every summer for most of the twentieth century.

At the end of his high school year in 1965, Max was impatient to get started on his chosen vocation of marine engineering. He applied to take a marine diesel course at the College of Trades and Technology in St. John's, but because mail service was just once a month on the Labrador Coast, Max was afraid his notification would come too late, so he decided to quit fishing early and, with $68 in his pocket, Max headed for St. John's on a government-run coastal boat that carried both freight and passengers.

Max encountered the first of several challenges that summer when, a few days into the voyage, he was told the ship would not be going to St. John's because longshoremen had gone on strike there, so he would have to get off in Lewisporte. As daunting as that was for a teenager who had never travelled much, Max made it to St. John's by train and found his way to the College, only to discover that his application had been refused because it arrived too late. However, the man in charge listened to Max's story and, "out of pity," according to Max, found a way to get around the issue and set the wheels in motion to have the young Labradorian enrolled at the College that is now known as the College of the North Atlantic.

"His name was Mr. Fiander and he asked me if I had enough money to live on while in St. John's. When I said I had about $50, Mr. Fiander said that wouldn't last long because room and board was expensive in the city," Max said.

"He sent me to Confederation Building, where I saw a couple of people, including one who arranged to have some money for me to get a bit of clothes. I guess I wasn't dressed too well.'"

He also discovered at Confederation Building that, because he was an orphan, he qualified for a larger monthly allowance than most students. Suddenly, between the jigs and the reels, things were starting to look up. Meanwhile, to come up with initial funding for his stay in the city, Max remembered that he had brought three seal skins with him from Labrador.

"There were three companies who bought seal skins in St. John's and I went to all three and then sold to the highest bidder, who offered me $20 each. So I had a few dollars in my pocket then," he laughs.

Completing the marine diesel course in St. John's was the beginning of a long and very successful career that led to many other courses to complete, until Max was qualified to be chief engineer on large oceangoing ships. In fact, Max's first job was on board the Coast Guard ship *John Cabot*, which was engaged in cable-laying duties between Europe and North America. Like most beginners, he started out as an oiler on the *Cabot*, but it wasn't long before he was moving up the ladder.

One of the make and break engines owned by Max

Max's career took him on a journey that saw him as engineer on cargo vessels, tankers, Coast Guard ships, private company vessels, and the famous Lake Boats on the Great Lakes. Those jobs took him to dozens of countries in Europe and Asia as well as North and South America.

Now in his sixties, Max is semi-retired and working a gig that most of us would consider a dream job. About fourteen years ago, Captain Lloyd Bugden from Newfoundland sold the ship *Duke of Topsail* to a company in the Bahamas to work as a local freighter. The Bahamian owners soon realized that while local engineers were competent to operate the engines on the *Duke*, maintenance and upgrading was outside their qualifications. The company approached Max and, after striking a deal, he started going south for several months a year and did maintenance work while the ship was still working. These days, he and his wife, Sandra (aka "Sugar"), still leave Newfoundland for the Bahamas in February for a couple of months and live on the ship while Max prepares the engines for another year.

"And you know what?" Max asks with a wry grin. "That ship has not missed a scheduled sailing in all those years due to mechanical trouble."

CHAPTER 17

Loss of the Pubnico Explorer

The weather in Meteghan, Nova Scotia, on Sunday evening, December 13, 2009, was fairly typical of late fall, early winter. It was cloudy with temperatures a few degrees above freezing.

The crew of the fishing vessel *Pubnico Explorer* had been busy preparing for what might be their last four- or five-day trip before Christmas that year. Leo Jeddry, the vessel's regular mate, took a look at the propeller shaft stuffing box because there had been considerable leakage in that area on recent trips.

Although Leo wouldn't be going with the boat on this upcoming trip because he was slated for a medical procedure, he worked on the stuffing box and secured all the fittings until there was no indication of water leaking in. He also helped the other crew members load the ice for their trip.

Caution was a good idea in the case of the *Pubnico Explorer*. Owned by Comeau Sea Products in Meteghan, the fifty-seven-foot Cape Island–style wooden boat was thirty years old and had taken on water a few times prior to 2009 that resulted in the captain making distress calls.

Pubnico Explorer

The first incident was on November 24, 2007. After receiving the distress call, a Coast Guard cutter brought pumps to get water from the hold and assisted the vessel back to port. According to a Transportation Safety Board (TSB) report, some hull repairs were carried out, but about two weeks later, on December 9, 2007, the *Pubnico Explorer* again transmitted a mayday due to what the report described as "a large ingress of water." Again, the same Coast Guard cutter went to the rescue and supplied pumps and the boat made it safely back to port.

The report states that in 2007 and 2008 the vessel underwent significant repairs, including re-sheathing a major portion of the hull, re-caulking the entire vessel, and installing a new pump manifold. It was generally accepted by everyone, including the Transportation Safety Board, that those repairs were sufficient to fix the damaged areas between the vessel's planks, where water was believed to be leaking in and caused the trouble during the 2007 incidents. And as far as anyone knows, it did.

But it seems that old boat problems can be like old habits—they don't give up easily, although this time the problem would arise in a different location on the boat.

Captain Dave Trask

According to the TSB report, a year or so after the refit the propeller stuffing box on the *Pubnico Explorer* started causing trouble. The report states: "The stuffing box had been leaking profusely during several trips before this one" [December 2009].

Satisfied that the stuffing box was in adequate condition and all other preparations were appropriately carried out, Captain David Trask gave the all-clear to ready for departure from Meteghan on Sunday evening. By Monday morning, the *Pubnico Explorer*, with Captain Trask, Relief Mate Neil Deveau, and two deckhands, was on the fishing grounds about fifty miles west of Meteghan at the mouth of the Bay of Fundy.

The crew fished for two days, and by Tuesday night they had landed approximately seventeen metric tons of redfish. At 5:00 a.m. on Wednesday, the company contacted the *Pubnico Explorer* to request a change of plans. A Comeau representative asked if the captain could head south to fish haddock.

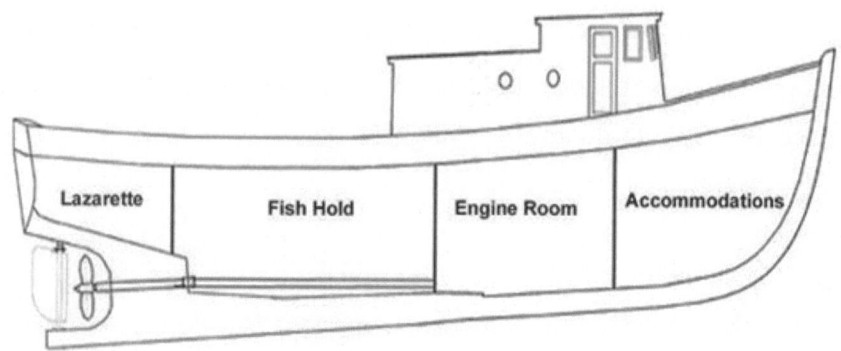

Architectural drawing of *Pubnico Explorer*

By nine o'clock, weather conditions had started deteriorating, so after making two tows for haddock, Captain Trask, a well-known and highly respected fisherman, decided it was time to head for port. They had landed only about one ton of haddock, not as much as he would have liked, but winds had picked up to forty knots from the northwest and seas were running twelve to fourteen feet high and increasing. Although the *Pubnico Explorer* had handled worse conditions on many occasions in its thirty-year life, the forecast called for worsening weather and it might become risky to continue fishing. After all, it was mid-December, and with the temperature now hovering around the freezing point, icing could become an issue with just a slight drop in temperature.

After the crew had hauled back the fishing gear and stowed the fish into the hold, the captain told the men to "go below" for a two-hour rest before they stowed the nets for the rest of the trip home to Meteghan. Captain Trask, a sixty-year old veteran fishing captain, took watch in the wheelhouse, expecting to be back in port at Meteghan by mid-afternoon that day.

When the three crew members went up on deck after their break, one of them noticed that the vessel was lower in the water, especially back aft, than when they had gone below two hours prior. Neil Deveau, an experienced fisherman, looked into the fish hold and became concerned when he saw about thirty centimetres (almost one foot) of water in the hold. He hurried to the wheelhouse to inform the skipper, who was unaware that the vessel had been taking on water. Apparently the highwater-level bilge alarms had been disconnected for some reason, and so there was no functional electronic system in place to send an alert of impending danger from the ingress of water below deck.

Captain Trask immediately went below to the engine room and turned on a bilge pump. According to the TSB report, Trask seemed overwhelmed when he returned to the wheelhouse: ". . . He appeared agitated and unwell; he was sweating and short of breath, with trembling legs and limited/impaired speech."

Meanwhile, the crew kept looking at the water level in the hold, and to their dismay it was rising despite the pump running.

Captain Trask remained in the wheelhouse and issued several instructions to address the problem, but Neil was unable to get the pump working at full capacity—the water was coming in at a rate greater than the pump could discharge. Water was also entering the engine room, but the level was controlled in that compartment by an electric bilge pump. The crew saw a small quantity of water in the lazarette, too, but they got a small sump pump in that area; after some initial difficulty, it began pumping water.

At 10:15 on Wednesday morning, Captain Trask called Marine

Communications and Traffic Services (MCTS) and asked for assistance. A few minutes later, he called MCTS again to ask for additional pumps. Shortly after that, he called a third time to say that there was no water in the engine room and he thought the vessel would be fine until a Coast Guard vessel or some other help arrived.

He was wrong.

A short while later, Captain Trask observed the rapid influx of water and he could no longer hope that everything was going to be all right. It was time that he and the three-man crew prepared for the worst. They didn't have to wait long before it happened.

With the water level steadily rising in two of the three below-deck compartments, the captain knew it was time to prepare to abandon ship.

Winds were from the northwest at approximately thirty-five knots (sixty-five kilometres), air temperature was at the freezing point, ocean temperature was also at zero degrees Celsius, seas were running three to four metres (ten to fourteen feet) and sometimes cresting much higher. After more than forty years at sea, Captain Trask knew those conditions meant trouble was at hand for a slowly sinking vessel.

Telling his crew members to "get their suits," one of the men hurried below to the accommodations quarters and came back to the wheelhouse with four immersion suits; they helped each other get them on. After overcoming some difficulty with fastening the zippers, Captain Dave Trask, Mate Neil Deveau, and crewmen Sydney Melanson and Peter Hogg were eventually suited up and ready to go over the side of their fishing vessel if necessary.

Sadly, their worries would come to fruition and abandoning ship would be more difficult than expected.

Shortly after 11:00 a.m., just as a crew member lowered another sump pump into the hold to try and contain the rise in water level, the men noticed that the stern of the vessel was now so low that ocean water was shipping in over the aft deck and running down the main hatch. It was now a matter of when, not if, the *Pubnico Explorer* would sink. Captain Trask gave the order to abandon ship.

One of the crewmen rushed to deploy the life raft, but it was too late. A couple of large waves struck the port side of the vessel and she began to list and roll heavily to starboard.

Not wanting to be in the wheelhouse or on deck when the vessel rolled over, Neil, Sydney, and Peter clambered up the port bulwark and jumped into the ocean. Captain Dave Trask was on deck, still near the wheelhouse door, but he didn't appear to make any attempt to follow his shipmates over the side.

Within moments after the three crewmen hit the cold ocean water, another large wave struck the port side of the *Pubnico Explorer* and finished her off. The fifty-seven-foot vessel capsized and sank about ten miles southwest of Meteghan.

It took a couple of minutes for Neil, Peter, and Sydney to fully assess what had just happened. All three were being tossed around in the heavy seas, making it difficult to communicate, especially in the high winds.

Although they knew that Search and Rescue had been alerted that their vessel had been taking on water, they were also aware that the last communication from Captain Trask indicated that he thought they were not in immediate danger of sinking, because the engine room was still fairly dry at the time. That was approximately forty-five minutes before the *Explorer* capsized.

The last time they saw the captain he was still standing outside the wheelhouse, so they were fairly certain he didn't have time to issue a final mayday.

They realized they were in big trouble if a rescue vessel didn't arrive quickly, but their luck took a turn for the better. The life raft that they didn't have time to manually deploy had a hydrostatic release system. That system activates a release mechanism when submerged in water and the raft capsule floats free of the vessel. When installed properly, the raft will inflate automatically with release. In this case, the canister released but, because the painter was not secured to the so-called "weak link," the raft did not inflate. But half a loaf is better than none, and when the canister containing the raft floated up, it drifted toward the men and came close enough to allow one of them to grab it. He pulled the painter and, to the relief of all three men, it worked. The six-man raft inflated, and within a couple of minutes they were safely inside.

The quick turn of events just before the capsizing meant that no one had time to release the emergency position-indicating radio beacon (EPIRB) either. An EPIRB is an electronic piece of equipment that activates when submerged and sends out a radio beacon to Search and Rescue (SAR) with its location.

However, once again luck was with the crew, and the EPIRB activated when the *Pubnico Explorer* went down. Search and Rescue picked up the location as 43.58.42N—66.24.18W. About twenty minutes later, the Canadian Coast Guard ship *Westport* pulled alongside and Neil, Sydney, and Peter were taken on board. All three were in good condition. The captain of the Coast Guard vessel decided to search for Captain Trask since it was obvious that the three crewmen didn't need immediate medical attention after their ordeal.

An extensive air and sea search for the missing skipper continued for the next twenty-four hours, including a US Coast Guard Falcon jet equipped with forward-looking infrared technology.

SAR operations were terminated about 1:00 p.m. on Thursday, December 17, and the case was passed over to the RCMP, who in turn put the case under a "missing persons" file.

In news reports on Thursday, Major James Simiana, with Joint Task Force Atlantic in Halifax, said the search area was hundreds of kilometres wide and had been "extensively gone over several times" by aircraft and the Coast Guard vessel as well as by local fishing vessels from the area.

"The determination has been made that at this point it would now be beyond the survival capability of the missing fisherman given the weather conditions that have prevailed since the ship sinking," he said.

On top of all that, it is believed that Captain Trask went down with the vessel inside the wheelhouse.

Why the captain didn't follow his three crew members who jumped overboard is unknown. One theory is that he may have tried to get back inside to issue a radio alert to Search and Rescue that they were abandoning ship. Another possibility is that he knew he was not physically able to climb up the port bulwark as the others did because of his health. The TSB report focused on his medical records and, along with much more, wrote: ". . . Although not indicated on the medical certificate, the master had, within the previous six months, taken prescription medication for the treatment of hypertension, chronic bronchitis, and emphysema."

Whatever the reason why he couldn't make it to the life raft, his fellow skippers in the area speak highly of Captain Trask's actions. Hubert Saulnier, a well-known captain in the region, says Trask did the job he was supposed to do.

"He made sure the crew were safe before he was going to leave—he's supposed to stay at the wheel, he's supposed to stay at the radio, contact the Coast Guard, assess the situation while the crew gets the life raft ready, survival suits, etc.—and they are the first ones to disembark from the boat. The captain did his job properly, from what I can see it's just very sad he didn't have time to make it out himself," says Saulnier.

Sad indeed.

From all accounts, the southwest Nova Scotia fishing industry lost a well-liked and respected man when Captain Dave Trask made his final voyage on December 16, 2009.

CHAPTER 18

Addicted to Fisheries

Glenn Blackwood is probably not an instantly recognizable name in every home in Newfoundland and Labrador—but it should be.

The native of Hare Bay, Bonavista Bay, has held the most prestigious positions with nearly every fisheries and marine agency in the province.

Today he is a vice-president of Memorial University of Newfoundland (Marine Institute), the largest university in Atlantic Canada and home to nearly 19,000 students. More than 1,000 of them are full-time students at the Institute.

But the reason Blackwood's personal profile is not as high as some people in lesser positions is because of his modesty. He has always wanted the PR focused on his projects rather than on himself.

A soft-spoken and friendly man, Blackwood beams when he reminisces about his childhood days in Hare Bay. He has fond memories of summer days out in a punt catching tomcods and flatfish and doing all the fun things that Newfoundland bay boys have done for centuries.

Blackwood is from a family of mariners. A couple of his uncles were fishermen, and his father worked on coastal boats along with his uncle, who was captain on one of the well-known passenger and freighting ships that served Newfoundland and Labrador coastal communities. As a child he hung around boats and wharves and cut out cod tongues to earn a bit of pocket money, so perhaps not surprisingly, young Glenn developed a curiosity about fish biology and decided that fisheries science would be his career choice.

Glenn Blackwood

During his university student days and then after graduation, Blackwood worked with provincial fisheries in the development branch. The job required a lot of travel, and he was having the time of his life.

"I spent my twenty-first birthday in Labrador on some river with Harry Martin."

Martin is a Labrador wildlife officer and better known as a great singer and songwriter.

Blackwood says that, as a people person, knowing so many wonderful folks in the fishing industry in his early career was a fascinating experience. He smiles as he remembers his association with names like Max Strickland from Burgeo, Frank Moore from Codroy, the Pateys of St. Anthony, and Lester Petten from Port de Grave, just to name a few.

Among other assignments, Blackwood worked on developing an eel fishery in Notre Dame Bay and lumpfish in Bonavista Bay. In fact, he wrote his honours dissertation on lumpfish.

In 1984, he became the "biologist" with the provincial department of fisheries and aquaculture and focused on growing the aquaculture industry, especially salmon farming on the south coast. Aquaculture is now worth tens of millions of dollars to the Newfoundland and Labrador economy.

In the late 1980s, Blackwood was appointed director for resource analysis, a position that required him to be part of federal and provincial committees responsible for fish assessments. That was just preceding the most calamitous event in Newfoundland and Labrador's fishery—the 1992 moratorium. In fact, it was in that capacity that Glenn Blackwood dared to officially suggest that northern cod might be in danger of collapse. The Department of Fisheries and Oceans Canada (DFO), which had the final say on science and management matters, did not take his argument seriously. He was a member of the Fisheries Resource Conservation Council (FRCC) and the Northwest Atlantic Fisheries Organization (NAFO) councils, and this gave him inside information not only on what Canada was thinking, but European countries as well. That was educational but sometimes frustrating.

Blackwood served as fisheries assistant deputy minister with the province for a little while, but he's not the political type, and soon he moved on to head up the Canadian Centre for Fisheries Innovation (CCFI) in 1997. Once again, he was happily working on projects for fishermen and marine people.

In 2000, he became the director of the Centre for Sustainable

Aquatic Resources (CSAR) at the Marine Institute, where he was responsible for the Institute's research and development activities related to harvesting and gear technologies and resource management.

Under his leadership, that Centre became a world leader in its field.

All that experience positioned Blackwood perfectly for the job that his colleagues say he was designed for. In 2005, he became director of the Marine Institute and is now vice-president.

Heading the Institute is the perfect fit for Blackwood's enthusiasm and passion for the fisheries and marine industries. Sit with him for a few minutes and it soon becomes obvious that talking about himself means talking about his work—not surprising, perhaps, when you consider all the great work that is going on at the Institute.

"Last year, we had students from every single province and territory in Canada," he says. "We graduate 400 students a year here, and in that sense that makes us the largest facility like this in the country."

Once portrayed as simply the cod college, the Marine Institute has grown to a centre for higher learning that now boasts several bachelor and masters degree programs. Blackwood is very happy to talk about how successful some of its graduates have become. For example, one Marine Institute graduate is first officer on one of the largest cruise ships in the world, while another has a major job with Disney Cruise Lines out of Florida. Others have attained highly successful careers in the offshore oil industry.

Having been on the front lines of the major changes to fisheries in the past thirty years, Blackwood has one pet peeve.

"We had one of the largest layoffs in Canadian history with the cod moratorium in 1992. Five years later, we had moved to mainly crab and shrimp. We shifted to new fishing gears, shifted to new markets, retrofitted vessels and fish plants, reopened groundfish plants to shrimp and crab facilities, and doubled the income [from fishing] to $1 billion a year up from $500 million. If that had happened to forestry in BC or agriculture on the prairies, it would have been hailed as the biggest success story in the history of the country. But not here," Blackwood says, obviously still frustrated by the fact that the fishing industry is still largely underplayed.

He says he understands people who point out that they couldn't accommodate all the 30,000 people who lost their jobs in 1992, but the fact that nearly half of them are still working in the industry, most with better pay, should be viewed as a matter of pride and not seen as a failure.

"Sometimes I say that I wish I wasn't addicted to the fisheries. But I am," he says, smiling.

Married and a father of two sons, Blackwood doesn't have a lot of spare time, but when he does get a few days off, he likes to spend time on the water. He has a couple of small pond boats, but his buddy in Lewisporte, Notre Dame Bay, has a powerboat, and they cruise around some of Newfoundland's many bays nearly every summer. His sons are accomplished hockey players, and chasing them around was almost a full-time job. He likes to go moose hunting when he can find time, but spending time with family and spending time in boats are what relaxes him best.

Glenn Blackwood's addiction to fisheries is not likely to diminish any time soon.

CHAPTER 19

The Memories Were All Made Here

Our *"Final Voyages"* stories have traditionally been about tragic loss of life at sea or the loss of a vessel that sank in the line of duty. A third criteria comes under the heading *"There but for the grace of God"*—meaning that there was no loss of life or vessel but an extremely close call.

In this chapter, I profile an esteemed fishing captain who made his final voyage in January 2014, but he *"crossed the bar"* on land after losing a year-long battle with cancer. Because Kevin Fiset was well-known for being more than just a fishing skipper and because he was an avid fan of the Navigator *magazine, especially the Final Voyages section, I gave the criteria some flexibility and decided to pay tribute to Kevin in the section of the magazine that his family says would surely receive Kevin's smiling stamp of approval.*

Kevin Fiset was born to be a fisherman. As a young lad growing up in the picturesque little town of Grand Etang on Cape Breton Island, Kevin's love for the sea and everything about it was obvious. In his early teens, Kevin and two of his buddies, Mark Larade and Jean-Guy Aucoin, built several model fishing vessels that were replicas of boats in the Grand Etang–Cheticamp area. The local newspaper *Inverness Oran* did a feature story with photos of the boys and their boats. It was about that time when Kevin started fishing with his grandfather every chance he'd get, and there was no question what his future vocation would be—he was a fisherman to the core.

Kevin chats with son Brendon on a leisurely summer's day on the water.
(Photo courtesy of Brenda Fiset Doucette)

Kevin's love of fishing was matched only by his passion for fishing vessels—everything from their design to their histories. His sister

Brenda (Fiset) Doucette, talks about all the "blue books" she remembers her brother had. Those blue books were Government of Canada registries of fishing vessels, and Kevin viewed them almost daily. His wife, Tammie, says he would even bring the books with him on family excursions around Cape Breton. Every time Kevin came across a boat he hadn't seen before, whether it was tied up at the wharf, at a Marine Service Centre, or in someone's backyard, he had to stop, size it up, and note the name, port of registry, and Commercial Fishing Vessel (CFV) number, along with his personal observations about the length, design, and anything else that caught his attention. Sometimes he'd have his blue book with him so he could cross-reference the details right on the spot, or he would write down the information to check on it when he returned home. All of this activity was often to the chagrin of his wife, Tammie, and especially his daughter Hailey. His son Brendon had an early interest in boats, but Tammie and Hailey were not overly excited about spending so much time sitting in the family vehicle waiting for Kevin to conduct his research.

"Sometimes it would take us hours to complete what would normally be a half-hour drive," Tammie remembers, smiling.

But Kevin couldn't really stop himself from indulging in his passion. In fact, in recent years it got more intense, especially with the introduction of good, inexpensive digital cameras. Kevin would snap pictures of boats from every angle to add to his already large and growing database of vessel photos to go along with the text data. Kevin shared many of those photos with his Facebook friends, and that would often prompt lengthy discussion among others.

When the government vessel registries went digital and the blue books were no longer published, Kevin got a computer and set it up in the corner of the living room in their modest home in Grand Etang to monitor every single entry. But his blue books remained close by for reference purposes long after the days of electronic registrations. Tammie has them all securely packed and stowed for safekeeping now.

Portrait of the Fiset family, 2006. Tammie, Kevin, Brendon, and Hailey (front). (Photo courtesy of Tammie Fiset)

It was Kevin's deep passion for detailed knowledge of fishing vessels that caught my attention. I became a Facebook friend of Kevin's several years ago, and it soon became obvious that this man had an enormous knowledge of every vessel, its owner, and history. If he didn't know, it was a challenge that had to be dealt with immediately, and an answer was usually found in short order. On a few occasions, Kevin's knowledge was a resource base for me at the *Navigator* when I needed information on a particular vessel. All I had to do was ask, and in jig time I had my reply.

Kevin was a quiet, kind, and unassuming man who also had a third passion. His love of family surpassed all else. Son of Aurel and Germaine, husband to Tammie and father of Brendon and Hailey, and brother to his only sibling, Brenda, Kevin was the consummate family man. He wasn't one for partying and crowds, but Kevin loved to cook and spend as much time with family as he could. Brenda says he was the classic "homebody."

Brendon's first trip to sea as captain of the *Hailey Dawn*, spring 2014
(Photo courtesy of Tammie Fiset)

"The memories were all made here," Tammie says in a phone conversation from her home. And it doesn't take long from chatting with her, Brendon, and Brenda to know that the memories are sweet and built on a foundation that will last forever.

Brenda, a teacher now living in Halifax, is very proud of her big brother.

"I've never known a man so proud to own a boat and earn a living from the sea," she poetically describes Kevin.

Kevin fished on a number of boats, including some in the offshore fishery, before purchasing his first vessel. He's from a family of sea people, including his dad, who is known as a top-notch diesel mechanic who practised his trade on board several vessels. Kevin also fished crab for several years but sold his snow crab licence after the crab resource declined.

Brendon has followed in his father's footsteps and went fishing whenever time would permit during his school days. He is twenty now and graduated from school.

Like his dad, Brendon is a soft-spoken young man who doesn't make a fuss about most things. He earned a reputation as a good hockey player in the midget league, but now that he's older, he has retired from the competitive leagues. His focus now is keeping his dad's dream alive.

Lobster trap buoy memorial Brendon made for his dad (Photo courtesy of Tammie Fiset)

Tammie is very happy that her young son has taken over for his dad and is keeping Kevin's beloved boat, *Hailey Dawn* (named after their daughter), and carrying on the family tradition. Although Brendon was young to take on the responsibility of operating a fishing enterprise and fishing a 39'11" vessel, he has a solid support system to back him up. Kevin's crewman for years stayed on and will be a major asset to Brendon.

Claude Deveau, a fellow skipper

from Grand Etang, a relative and close friend of Kevin's, stated it well. Claude said there are about twenty boats fishing from that harbour and, in a small community like Grand Etang, everyone is like family.

"We'll all be there for Brendon for as long as it takes."

With a support system like that, empires can be built, let alone a small fishing enterprise.

Hailey is now fifteen and is a vibrant teenager who is very involved in a number of artistic interests including dance.

Something tells me that I haven't heard the last of the fishing name Fiset of Grand Etang for a long, long time. I wish them the very best of everything.

CHAPTER 20

Take Care of Your Mother

The cod moratorium that stunned Newfoundland and Labrador fishermen in July 1992 didn't put an end to tragedy in the province's inshore fishery.

Barely a month after the moratorium went into effect, the small fishing community of St. Lewis–Fox Harbour, Labrador, was shocked by the loss of two of its fishermen.

Caplin were plentiful on the Labrador Coast that summer, and on August 11, just a little over a month after the cod fishery was shut down, Ed Poole, his father, Earl, and cousin Wallace left their summer fishing station in Murray's Harbour to haul a caplin net in nearby Crow Bay.

That fateful Wednesday started out as a beautiful morning. It was sunny and warm, although there was a "bit of a breeze from the southwest," as Ed described it.

The three men were delighted to see that their net was full of caplin.

"Boys, there's enough caplin here to feed everyone in Fox Harbour all winter," Wallace joked as they started hauling the net over the side of the boat.

Ed was in the back of the speedboat, and shortly after Wallace's upbeat comments he noticed lops splashing over the stern.

"I said to Dad and Wallace that a fair bit of water was coming in, but I don't know if they heard me or not because they didn't look back but just kept on hauling more net and more caplin on board."

Perhaps Earl and Wallace were not worried about anything because, even though it was only eighteen feet, their boat was a flat-bottom design and very sturdy. Ed's brother Fred says he remembers, when the boat was new, they were testing it out and they were surprised that four or five men could stand on the gunwales and the boat would hardly list at all.

Aeriel view of Fox Harbour–St. Lewis (Photo courtesy of Calvin Poole)

But somehow this time was different, and soon Ed realized that the amount of water coming in was worrisome. He tried bailing out the water, but it was a losing battle as more water was coming in than he could handle. That's when Ed realized they were in big trouble.

"I shouted to the others to move to the front because the stern was almost underwater."

His father and Wallace looked back and for the first time realized that the boat was half-submerged. As Ed suggested, they moved toward the bow, but the attempt to level the water inside the boat from back to front was too late and the little boat continued filling with more water.

Ed says he recalls that someone seemed to move too quickly and, suddenly, the boat capsized and all three were thrown overboard.

Ordinarily, getting thrown overboard in the circumstances the Poole men found themselves in that morning would not appear to be very serious. Despite the fact that Ed was the only one wearing a life jacket and the only one who could swim, the boat was only ten feet from shore. In fact, the net was tied to the rocks. What could go wrong? It was a warm day in summer, so it should have been just a matter of one of them getting ashore and throwing a line to the others, and the day should have ended with the men getting no more than a good soaking.

But the ocean doesn't always behave the way we think it should and, as often happens in times of crisis, people are not always certain about how and why some things occur.

For example, Ed remembers that when he surfaced near the boat, he grabbed his father and kept him close at hand, but at first he couldn't see any sign of Wallace.

"I looked out to the southeast and there he was, about ten fathoms [sixty feet] away from us. I shouted at him and said, 'How the hell did you get out there? Come back in out of it!'"

Wallace heard his cousin and looked at Ed, and in a motion that resembled an attempt to walk rather than swim, he suddenly sank beneath the surface.

That was the last time anyone ever saw Wallace alive.

Because Ed was wearing a flotation device, it's likely that he wasn't underwater for any longer than a few seconds. His dad, on the other hand, was not wearing a life jacket and had big rubber boots on that were filled with water, pulling him down. Eventually, Ed saw his dad underwater, pulled him to the surface, and starting pushing him toward the side of the overturned speedboat. By then Earl was already fatigued, confused, and likely suffering from water ingestion.

He seemed to know that he might not make it.

Looking at his son, Earl said, "Ed, take care of your mother."

Just minutes later, Ed Poole realized that Earl had succumbed and there was nothing he could do except hold onto the boat with one hand and keep a firm grasp on his dad's coat for fear of having him slip under the surface and losing him.

As the boat drifted away from the shoreline, Ed tried to remain focused and figure out a plan to save his own life.

Looking to see if there were any other boats in the vicinity, he saw several whales inching closer and closer toward him, as if they were curious about what was going on. "I looked up to the sky and I said, 'Well, well . . . here I am up to my neck in water and now I got to deal with friggin' whales.'"

The whales kept their distance, but Ed had other issues to deal with.

Although the air temperature might have been warm, the water was very cold. He noted that there were seven icebergs in Crow Bay that morning, and the boat was drifting straight toward one. He wondered whether he'd try and get on a berg if the boat came close enough but worried that it might even be colder on the ice than in the water. He didn't have to make the decision.

"Something strange happened. The boat was headed for the ice, but suddenly she took a turn and moved away and circled around, almost as if someone took her in tow or something," he says.

Fox Harbour–St. Lewis (Photo courtesy of Calvin Poole)

Meanwhile, back in Murray's Harbour, Ed's mom was anxiously glancing at the kitchen clock. Earl had told her that they'd be back by ten o'clock, but it was almost noon.

They should be back by now, she thought. She wondered if the men were having engine trouble. She contacted Tom Holley, a family friend, who knew exactly where the Pooles' caplin net was, and he left immediately to check on his friends. At first there was no sign of the Pooles' boat, but as he drew nearer to their net, he saw a flash—like sunlight reflecting from a mirror. In later chats about the events of that day, Tom and Ed figured that what Tom saw was a reflection of the sun on Ed's sunglasses.

Whatever it was, it gave Tom cause to take a closer look, and a minute later he saw Ed, still clinging to his father's jacket with one hand and the overturned boat with the other.

Fortunately, Tom Holley was a big, strong man. Otherwise, it would have difficult to get Earl and Ed from the water into his boat. He managed to haul Earl in first and then got Ed on board. Tom says Ed was groggy and wanting sleep, but he started to come around once on board the speedboat.

It was miraculous that all he felt was groggy. They figured Ed had been in the ice-infested ocean for about two hours and twenty minutes before Tom showed up. Ordinarily, most people would have been in an advanced state of hypothermia within twenty to twenty-five minutes, but somehow Ed Poole is different than most people and is still alive to tell the tale.

Wallace's body was recovered the next day, and although fishing communities have long been accustomed to tragedy at sea, the shock and sorrow is no less crushing when it happens to your own.

August 11, 1992, will be long remembered by folks in Murray's Harbour and St. Lewis–Fox Harbour, Labrador, as the day that fifty-nine-year-old Earl Poole and his thirty-year-old nephew, Wallace Poole, made their final voyage.

CHAPTER 21

The Harbour Manager

Floyd d'Entremont is probably the most recognizable name in the Pubnico area of southwestern Nova Scotia. In a region where there are hundreds of d'Entremonts and perhaps even another Floyd or two, if you ask for information on Floyd d'Entremont, chances are you will get a response that goes something like, "You mean Floyd the harbour manager, right?"

Floyd d'Entremont has been Harbour Manager of the Dennis Point Wharf in West Pubnico, southwestern Nova Scotia, for more than twenty years. He is well-known because Dennis Point–West Pubnico is one of the largest fishing ports in Nova Scotia, possibly the largest, which in turn would make it one of the largest fishing ports in all of Canada.

Close to eighty-five lobster-vessel owners and captains call it home port. About twenty draggers, several seiners, and a few other vessel types in the home fleet mean that Dennis Point is very diversified and, as such, the port operates year-round because in southwest Nova Scotia one or more fish species are landed every week of the year.

Floyd is an affable fellow who looks younger than his fifty years. His positive demeanour is not just with his clients and friends. Floyd is a person who, when you first meet, you wish you could have more of his time to chat. I remember one fall afternoon a couple of years ago standing and chatting with Floyd on the parking lot next to the Harbour Authority office. Floyd was giving me a basic lesson in his native Acadian French language and how it differs from the Montreal French dialect.

Floyd d'Entremont

"Acadian French is easier for non–French speaking people to learn," he says.

His zest for life is evident even during casual conversation and makes you want to stay and hear much more than his busy schedule and his constantly ringing cellphone will allow.

Besides being Harbour Manager for the past twenty-four years, Floyd operates a lobster buying company that he's had for over thirty years. Going back even before that, he worked on the *Bluenose*—not the world-famous racing schooner, but the Bar Harbor–Yarmouth ferry of the same name.

"It was just summer jobs back then. It was fun and they paid good money, too," he laughs.

His father was a long-time fisherman who fished until he was seventy-three or seventy-four, but Floyd was not attracted to a life on the sea. He did fish one season with his dad, but after a couple of bouts of seasickness, he decided that he'd better look for something different. Ironically, Floyd says his first job was at the wharf that he now manages.

"I was thirteen and Digby scallopers would land there and they needed shuckers, so I did that for a while in the summer."

Floyd is a proud French Acadian who is very happy at home in Lower West Pubnico.

"I was born and raised here and I've never been away from here for more than eleven days at one time. It's crazy," he says, laughing heartily at himself, knowing that for someone of his resources, people look at him curiously when he makes that statement. "I do travel a bit, but we just don't stay for long. The longest vacation I ever had was when we went to a wedding in Boston once, and afterwards we went to Cape Cod and made a bit of a holiday out of it. These days, my son, who is twenty-two, works out west in the oil business, so we go out there."

Even when asked what he likes most about the job as Harbour Manager, Floyd doesn't hesitate for a second: "Because it's home," he says, smiling.

Other than working at home, Floyd likes the job for the very reason that it would scare away some people. "I don't work scheduled hours— I'm at the wharf almost every day because we have boats coming and going every week of the year and at all times of the day and night, so I'm not working nine to five and I like that," he says. "The wharf is also my social life. I know almost every captain and most of their crews and I really enjoy talking to them all."

As is prevalent in the French Acadian culture, family is extremely important to Floyd. The father of a son and daughter, he talks proudly of his children and has fond memories of focusing his attention on their upbringing. He says he and his wife were constantly on the road with the children, going to sporting events all over the province and even outside Nova Scotia.

"We focused everything on giving them every opportunity we could." Some parents make that statement sound like it was a chore, but not Floyd d'Entremont. It's obvious that he and his wife enjoyed every minute of it and, in fact, are very thankful that they were so fortunate to have the opportunity and wouldn't hesitate to do it all again.

Despite having a twenty-four-hour workday, seven days a week, Floyd also finds time to relax and indulge in one of his personal pleasures. "I play guitar and sing just about every day," he says. He also does a little bit of songwriting and will sing and play publicly if anyone asks.

One of his four older sisters, Rowena, says Floyd is a good singer and also a really good songwriter and that music is an important part of her brother's life. She says Floyd is playing and singing more and more in public these days, in venues like farmer's markets and small restaurants.

In his other day job, Floyd is a lobster buyer for the De La Tour Co-op. The company has operated for more than seventy years, making it one of the oldest businesses in the region. The company is named after Charles de la Tour, the founder. Floyd speaks with a tone of pride and almost reverence in his voice when he talks about the co-op, where he is also a member. At one point he referenced the co-op as a "movement" when describing its origins and how he worked there for a while many years ago as a clerk. He is happy to explain how it grew from a small business starting in a tiny building to become a large and diversified company.

"The lobster sector of the company is owned by fishermen only, but the store, hardware, lumber, and petroleum sectors are owned by all community members," he explains, adding that they are now even licensed to sell liquor. "My grandfather was a founding member of one sector."

Co-operatives are popular in southwest Nova Scotia and seem a natural fit in the Acadian French culture and their strong sense of community and family.

Floyd d'Entremont, the harbourmaster, is a very positive example of that culture.

CHAPTER 22

The Last of His Era

Captain Les McCarthy boasts a stellar marine and fishing career that is ongoing. At sixty-eight, he's fished for more than fifty years and has commanded vessels for about forty-eight of those years. That impressive bio makes him the senior captain of the west coast Newfoundland herring seine fleet and perhaps in all of Atlantic Canada. But mere statistics do not make anyone exceptional. Les McCarthy has also earned utmost respect and admiration for his fisheries knowledge, fishing abilities, and leadership qualities. He is a master at his craft.

Bill Barry has known Les since he was a boy. The head of the Barry Group of Companies based in Corner Brook is seldom at a loss for words, but when asked for some thoughts about his lifelong friend, he

189

stumbles trying to find the proper language to adequately express his admiration and respect for Les.

"I think the world of him. I couldn't speak more highly of anyone from a professional standpoint, but also as a person in the general sense as well. He is a magnificent character."

Barry says Captain Les has an intuitive and unique ability to land herring when others sometimes struggle.

"Even his colleagues and peers will tell you that Les is probably the best shoal-water seiner in the business. He can catch herring in those conditions like none other and not damage the seine. He is in a class by himself that way," Barry says. "He is the essence of a professional—the fellow that you want in the wheelhouse for any and every occasion—the one you'd want to send your kids to sea with to learn the business because he's the best of the best."

Captain Les McCarthy in the wheelhouse of the seiner *Ocean Leader*

Les is from a long line of herring fishermen. His ancestors from the Terrenceville and English Harbour East areas of Fortune Bay suffered a multi-year catch failure around the turn of the twentieth century. Several seiners started travelling to Labrador in the first few years of the 1900s to participate in the cod fishery, but they still needed herring for bait. The best herring fishery at that time was on Newfoundland's west coast. After several seasons of going to Bay of Islands to fish herring and then continuing on to Labrador, several of the traditional herring fishermen decided to pull up stakes in Fortune Bay altogether and settled their families on the west coast to do what they knew best: herring seining. Woods Island, located at the mouth of the Bay of Islands, was their chosen new home, and soon well-known Fortune Bay names like McCarthy, Hackett, and Hickey were west coast seining masters. Today, Les McCarthy is the last of his era, but his son will likely succeed him when Les retires.

Les practically learned to walk on the deck of a seiner. His father, Mike, was also a well-known captain. In my book *Sea Folk*, I published a story about Captain Mike McCarthy's death in January 1980. Captain Mike was boarding his seiner one winter's night in North Sydney when he fell between his vessel and the wharf and perished.

Les has fond memories of being on board vessels with his dad as a young boy. Knowing that he would be following in his father's footsteps, Les was carefully watching and learning his future craft at an elementary-school age. His early work experiences were with his father on board collector boats that travelled up and down the Labrador Coast collecting fish from small boat fishermen and then transporting it back to the island for processing. While still a teenager he went to Cape Breton working as a crew member on fishing draggers. By the time he turned twenty, he had impressed company owners enough that they offered Les his first full-time position as captain.

"That was on the *Alder Point*, an eighty-seven-foot side dragger in Cape Breton," Les says.

A couple of years later, he returned to Newfoundland, alternating between collectors and seiners before eventually becoming exclusively involved in the herring seiner fishery.

By the time Les was in his thirties, he had advanced in his trade to a point that he was leading and conducting research work for the Newfoundland Government on the province's east coast. Government wanted to determine if purse seining for herring was feasible on the east coast of Newfoundland in large vessels, because east coast fishermen had traditionally fished herring with fixed gear, but seining was more efficient. Les was captain of the National Sea seiner *Canada 100*, a 100-foot vessel, and he says their survey work demonstrated that all east coast bays could easily support seine technology at that time.

Ocean Leader docked at Barry's Fisheries, Corner Brook

It is interesting to listen to Les's take on the state of today's herring stock on the west coast of Newfoundland and in the Gulf of St. Lawrence. There have been significant changes over the past twenty years, according to Les. He says there are just as many herring in his zone today as there ever were, but he thinks their behaviour has changed. He says years ago herring would appear in one area at a time and then migrate from one bay to the other. Now he says they show up in all the bays on the west coast at the same time.

Herring spawning behaviour has changed, too, he says. Traditionally, herring had two spawning seasons in his area—spring and fall—but he thinks that the stock now spawn mostly in fall. And not only has their spawning time changed, Les says herring are spawning much farther to the west, nearer to Quebec than Newfoundland. However, they still travel over the same grounds, but in broader aggregations and at different times of year.

Les is a soft-spoken man who answers questions directly and honestly. He smiled when asked if he has any plans for retirement.

"Not really," he said. "As long as I feel good and in good health, I see no reason to give it up yet. In fact, I feel like I'm sort of semi-retired anyway these days because government regulations keep us tied up at the wharf half the time."

Les explains that, during his early years, seiners worked year-round and were allowed in most of Atlantic Canadian waters. Now, he says, they are only allowed in certain areas at specific times of the year, they are not allowed to fish in certain depths of water, and they are restricted to waters, more or less, next door to home. It's when he talks about those layers of bureaucratic policies that you see a rare flash of frustration in the otherwise calm and cool captain. He explains how many of the Ottawa-designed rules are made by people who wouldn't know a herring from a hippopotamus.

"In many cases they [the people and the rules] make no sense at all," he says, admitting, though, that a lot of fisheries policies are tied to politics as much as science. One of his pet peeves is a policy that says he must fish in two or more zones to take fish that are part of the same stock. He raises a valid point. If he has a quota of 100 fish from the same aggregation, why does he have to fish fifty of them in Box A and then have to travel to Box B before he can take the second half of his allowance?

This frustration with the bureaucracy is not uncommon these days. Many retirements are decided for that reason rather than based on economics or age. However, frustrations aside, Les will not take the decision to retire without a lot of soul searching. The sea and the art of fishing have always defined who and what he is for his entire life. It's in his blood and at the core of his entire existence. For a man like Les, that essence is not easily transferred from the wheelhouse to spending mornings at Tim Hortons.

CHAPTER 23

The Worst Day of My Life

On Tuesday morning, May 3, 2011, Raymond "Ray" Belliveau arrived at his harbourfront office in Lower East Pubnico at seven thirty, about the same time he arrived most mornings. The owner of Charlesville Fisheries Ltd. in southwest Nova Scotia liked to get an early start on his workday because managing a fish plant as well as coordinating a fleet of five inshore draggers required long, busy hours, especially during, or preparing for, peak fishing seasons.

For the most part, things looked normal as Ray pulled alongside the harbourfront that morning, although he noticed his vessel *Silver Angel* was not at the dock as he had expected. The fifty-eight-foot vessel left East Jeddore near Halifax on Monday morning and was scheduled to arrive at East Pubnico late that night or early Tuesday morning to undergo a scheduled Transport Canada inspection. Because the vessel was going to be out of service for a few days, one of the *Silver Angel*'s crew members was to drive his vehicle to East Pubnico and meet his fellow crewmate Ward Wickens and Captain Gerry Henneberry. Once the vessel was secured, the three men planned to drive back to their homes in, or near, East Jeddore while the inspections were under way.

Silver Angel

At first Ray didn't think much about it. Boats often get delayed for a variety of reasons. Still, the first thing he did once inside the office was check the *Silver Angel*'s location. He checked the vessel's so-called black box reading and noticed the coordinates indicated the *Silver Angel* was about five and a half nautical miles off Cape Sable Island and apparently not moving.

"I still didn't think it was anything serious at first," Ray says, but he was wrong.

At ten o'clock on Monday morning, Captain Gerry Henneberry and Ward Wickens pulled away from the wharf in East Jeddore and headed the *Silver Angel* on a southwesterly course toward the Pubnicos.

It was a fairly routine and uneventful day, and by 11:00 p.m. the *Silver Angel* was only a few hours from reaching its destination.

Just before midnight, the northeast wind increased to about thirty knots and the vessel was rolling about twenty-five degrees, so the captain decided to deploy the paravane stabilizers to allow for a smoother trip. The stabilizers are triangular pieces of metal attached to a chain and lowered under water by booms stretching out from the vessel's sides. Once submerged, the kite-shaped paravanes slice through the ocean and keep the vessel from rolling heavily.

At about midnight, the two men had the stabilizers secured and went back inside. Gerry said he would take a nap and handed the watch over to Ward, asking to be called when they were about five nautical miles south of Cape Sable Island. Gerry knew the area well and told Ward he wanted to retrieve both stabilizers before entering waters where lobster trap buoys could get snagged in them. Gerry then went to his bunk for a much-needed rest.

At 4:45 a.m., the vessel was south of Cape Sable Island and Ward called out to inform Gerry that it was time to retrieve the stabilizers. The captain went to the wheelhouse and took the vessel out of gear while Ward went aft to work on the port paravane. Both men had done this procedure on numerous occasions, and this time it was no different. After smoothly going through all the motions of getting everything ready for the final steps in securing the paravanes on board, Gerry moved to the starboard side of the upper deck, let go the starboard paravane rope from the cleat, and looked aft to check on Ward, who would normally be near the starboard aft gantry.

He couldn't see Ward, but that didn't worry him because he knew Ward was very efficient and he assumed his thirty-three-year-old deckhand had moved on and was waiting for the line just aft of the upper deck.

With that thought, Gerry began crawling back on top of a row of tote boxes to pass the line to Ward. That's when Gerry's heart started pumping like crazy. He saw Ward in the water about nine or twelve feet off the vessel's side, just forward of the starboard aft gantry. Ward was calling out for help. Gerry quickly climbed back off the boxes and secured the starboard paravane line on its cleat to steady the vessel. Running as fast as he could through the wheelhouse, down the stairwell, and out onto the back deck, Gerry grabbed a gaff from the starboard side of the net reel on the stern and attempted to reach Ward with it, but the gaff wasn't long enough. Gerry then ran forward, took a life ring from its bracket on the starboard side, rushed back aft, and without uncoiling the rope he threw the ring with the line as hard as he could toward Ward. It fell several feet short.

He ran forward again and picked up a coil of 3/8-inch rope, but when he reached the stern section of the boat again, Gerry froze in his tracks—he could no longer see Ward.

Being the only one on board the fifty-eight-foot vessel meant that manoeuvring the boat and hurrying around the decks in the dark took time. Although Gerry knew his boat well and moved with good speed, time was running out. He ran to the wheelhouse and, at 4:58 a.m., sent a frantic distress signal on channel 16 very high frequency (VHF) radio advising that he had a man in the water in position latitude 44°18'42"N and longitude 65°41'18"W.

Gerry was a seasoned captain, and although his heart raced he was still in control of his emotions, and he continued to do what he had been trained to do in situations like this. He put the *Silver Angel*'s engine in gear and started searching for Ward, hoping for the best but also knowing that, without a life jacket or any flotation device, Ward was in serious trouble in the frigid waters off Nova Scotia in May.

Gerry's frantic mayday call transmitted successfully, and fishing boats in the area immediately swung their bows toward the location of the *Silver Angel*. Within minutes they were on the way to assist Gerry in the search. A Cormorant helicopter and two Coast Guard ships later joined the two dozen fishing boats and spent a day searching the waters for Ward Wickens—sadly, without success. The life ring that Gerry had thrown to his deckhand was recovered, but there was no sign of Ward.

When fishermen die at sea, it is often difficult for loved ones to find closure because, in many incidents, the body is never recovered. For long agonizing days, weeks, and months, those left behind grieve, but still cling to a tiny shred of hope that their son, husband, or brother made it to safety somehow.

In small fishing communities, everyone is touched because, besides the immediate family members, the entire town is extended family.

It was exactly that way when thirty-three-year-old Ward Wickens fell overboard from the fishing vessel *Silver Angel* near Cape Sable Island, Nova Scotia, on May 3, 2011. He was never seen again and an entire community mourned deeply.

Ray Belliveau was one of those grief-stricken people.

"It was the worst day of my life," he says.

Ray's company, Charlesville Fisheries, owned the *Silver Angel*, and Ward was both an employee and a friend.

Some things about that day still seem surreal to Ray, but he remembers that the *Silver Angel* and Captain Gerry Henneberry arrived at the dock in East Pubnico at ten o'clock that Tuesday morning. Ray went on board to talk to the captain of his vessel to learn more about the accident and also to try and help Gerry.

"I did all I could to comfort Gerry—he was not in a good state," Ray recalls.

Comforting Gerry was one thing, but when Ray received confirmation from search officials that there was no hope of finding Ward alive, he knew the worst was yet to come. He knew he had to drive to Bear Point, Shelburne County, to talk to Dana Wickens, Ward's wife.

"She already knew that Ward was gone, but I had to go anyway. It was just the right thing to do," Ray says, adding that not a single day has passed since May 3, 2011, that Ward hasn't crossed his mind.

His mind racing wildly with emotions and fears, Ray asked a friend, who was also a fishing captain, to go to Bear Point with him. They left East Pubnico and drove through the fishing villages of Woods Harbour and Shag Harbour before finally arriving at Bear Point.

"We arrived there around noon. I can't tell you what that was like—it was tough," Ray said. "All I could do was express my sympathy and offer any help that was required."

And he did help. Ray won't disclose the amount because it is a private matter, but he has contributed financially to Dana and her family.

Two Transportation Safety Board of Canada investigators came to East Pubnico that week and checked out the boat. Everything on the *Silver Angel* complied with Transport Canada regulations, but Ray soon learned that the Nova Scotia Labour Department also had jurisdiction over occupational health and safety in the fishing industry. Like most other vessel owners and fishermen in his region, Ray was not aware of that, but it soon became apparent that his company, Charlesville Fisheries, was deemed to be at fault under the Nova Scotia Occupational

Health and Safety Act regulations, and the company's health and safety program had to be modified.

On December 19, 2012, Charlesville Fisheries Ltd. pleaded guilty to committing an offence contrary to the part of the Occupational Health and Safety Act that requires employers to ensure that their fishermen wear personal protective equipment while working. Ward Wickens was not wearing a personal flotation device (PFD) when he fell overboard from the *Silver Angel*.

Ray Belliveau addressing an audience in Moncton about the importance of safety and knowing safety rules and regulations and vessel owner responsibility

Despite the fact that Ray Belliveau's company had been in total compliance with Transport Canada's rules, and even though Ray voluntarily committed to make financial contributions to Dana Wickens, the court had no choice but to sentence Charlesville Fisheries. However, the judge found a "creative" way of penalizing the company.

It became obvious during court proceedings that Ray Belliveau was not the only vessel owner who was unaware that provincial health and safety regulations overrode Transport Canada's requirements, or even what those regulations were—far from it. In fact, it's believed that a sizable majority of vessel owners were unaware of it. The judge realized that an education program was needed, and as part of the sentence Charlesville Fisheries was ordered to make a donation to the Fisheries Safety Association of Nova Scotia. The company also received a fine, but the judge took into account the fact that Charlesville Fisheries provided financial assistance to the family of Ward Wickens.

But the financial costs didn't end by paying a fine. Ray won't say how much he voluntarily paid to the Wickens family, but a huge increase in insurance premiums and Workers' Compensation Board payments on all five of his vessels has cost his company in excess of $250,000.

But perhaps the most creative penalty the court added to the company's sentencing was ordering Ray Belliveau to make three public presentations outlining what went wrong on the morning that Ward Wickens died and what could have prevented the accident.

As difficult as it was for the soft-spoken Ray Belliveau to stand in front of three separate audiences and discuss the details of the worst day of his life, he embraced the concept.

"Even without the court requirement, I wouldn't have any problem doing those presentations," Belliveau said during his first talk in Digby. "This is something I believe very strongly in. Hopefully no one else in Nova Scotia ever has to go through what the Wickens family, and we, went through."

I attended Ray's presentation to an audience during the Fish Canada Workboat Canada show in Moncton in January 2013. He has long finished his three required presentations, but his sincerest hope now is to do everything he can to prevent another death at sea that doesn't have to happen. Driven by that inner conviction, Ray will sit and talk with anyone who will listen.

Listening to Ray talk about the accident, one is struck by his sincerity, modesty, and integrity. It is easy to tell the man is still dealing with the hurt of losing Ward Wickens, and as he goes through the details, one can't help but feel his personal pain. Speaking softly, he explains how Captain Gerry Henneberry was unable to conduct an effective rescue mission for Ward because it was impossible to manoeuvre a large vessel and be in all the right places to get a man overboard back on the boat.

Ward was not wearing a personal flotation device of any kind, and though it is impossible to force crew members to wear PFDs at sea, Ray has made it mandatory as his company's new safety policy, and there will be consequences if a crew member is found in contravention of the policy. On the first infraction they will be given a severe reprimand, and on the second they will be fired.

He also has made it mandatory to have at least three people on his vessels at any time. Company vessels also now have ladders on board that can be placed over the rails of the boat to help retrieve individuals who have fallen overboard. He has also posted notices on his vessels indicating that wearing a PFD is mandatory.

"We never felt we were operating our vessels in an unsafe manner, although we actually were," Belliveau said. He adds, "We were woefully unprepared with only two men aboard. Once Ward went overboard, it was impossible for Gerry to operate the vessel and keep Ward in sight, especially as he wasn't wearing a PFD."

In a report, the Transportation Safety Board said that, from 2000 to

2011, it recorded forty-seven fatalities involving crew members falling overboard out of a total of 153 fishing boat deaths. If Ray Belliveau gets his way, those numbers will be significantly lower in the next eleven years.

CHAPTER 24

Fishing and Fancy Cars

"I have my own town—Saulnierville." That's how Hubert Saulnier from Saulnierville, Nova Scotia, jokingly responds sometimes when strangers ask where he's from.

Saulnierville is a picturesque French Acadian community in southwest Nova Scotia, about a twenty-minute drive north of Yarmouth. From a long line of fishing families, Hubert is one of the best-known fishermen in his area. The fifty-nine-year-old has always been an active community and industry supporter. Among other positions, he is president of the Maritime Fishermen's Union (MFU) local in his region. He dreams of uniting fishermen in southwest Nova Scotia in a more powerful unit, similar to the Fish, Food & Allied Workers (FFAW) in Newfoundland and Labrador, where the union represents and speaks for fishermen with collective bargaining certification to negotiate fish prices and other matters on behalf of all fishermen in the province. In Nova Scotia, the MFU doesn't have mandatory dues rights and can only speak for those who voluntarily pay membership fees. Nova Scotia fishermen also have about sixty regional associations scattered throughout the province. Hubert believes the larger, single-unit model would work better for fishermen because of the strength-in-numbers concept. But Hubert has an interesting philosophy on growing the union.

Hubert Saulnier

"We don't go knocking on doors looking for new members. I'd rather have a smaller number who believe in the cause and who want to work hard for the union than have a huge number of people who don't want to be there. That doesn't work."

Besides the MFU, Hubert is part of many other groups, including the Marine Rescue Auxiliary (Coast Guard), Fundy Fixed Gear Council, the Council of Canadian Professional Fish Harvesters, and he serves on the LFA 34 advisory committee. He is also involved with a couple of organizations in Maine. Lobster fishermen there may be from a different country, but they have a lot in common, in some cases sharing the same lobster stocks.

Hubert is often called on to speak at fisheries forums around the country. He enjoys that because, after he has his say, he likes to stay around and listen to all the other guests.

"That's how you learn things. I could fly in and do my thing and leave again, but if I'm the only person I hear speak, I don't learn anything new and there's always plenty more to learn no matter how long you've been around," he says.

Hubert comes from a long lineage of fishermen. He fished with his father when he was just a boy and, as the oldest of nine children, Hubert more or less had to quit school at age fifteen to fish full-time with his dad in order to make ends meet for their large family.

"Times were harder back then. We would fish in season and work up in Greenwood or somewhere later because there was no EI or other social programs like there are now."

Like most fishermen in those days, Hubert remembers working on a credit system with the merchants.

"Some weeks you'd have a bit of money left after the bills were paid, but sometimes you'd wind up owing them and we would have to go without any money for a week or two. It was tough," he says.

It was also tough to make a living working in fish plants back then, too. When he wasn't fishing, Hubert sometimes worked in a plant when he was young.

"I was making one dollar an hour, and when I got married they gave me a raise—I got $1.25 an hour then."

Although times were hard, Hubert liked the life on the water and was determined to make it pay. He bought his first boat in 1973, and then, two years later, when his father sold his licence to the government in a buyback program, Hubert purchased his dad's boat.

"My father got $6,000 for his license," Hubert says with a chuckle, realizing how much more that licence could fetch today. "That was the rate back then—$6,000 for an active licence and $2,000 for an inactive one."

He remembers borrowing $6,600 to start up his own fishing enterprise. Young people would scoff at such a low sum today, but as he points out, servicing a $6,000 debt left very little money for him and his crew in the 1970s.

Over his more than forty years in the business, Hubert fished several species but, like most southwest Nova Scotia fishermen, he is primarily a lobsterman these days and lives a much more comfortable lifestyle than he could have thirty or forty years ago.

There's more to Hubert Saulnier than fishing and serving on associations. He also has a passion for old cars. He owns three antiques that he loves to tell you about. He has a motorcycle that he won in a ticket draw, and he has two sports cars. His 1966 Pontiac Parisienne is in mint condition.

"You can still see the serial number on the engine." Powered by a 327 V8, it's a large vehicle that glides like an airplane, Hubert says.

He also owns a 1970 Pontiac GTO Judge. With a 455-horsepower engine, that car is very fond of gas.

"It can only get twelve miles to the gallon," he says, smiling. He adds that he rarely takes it out of the garage except for an occasional short ride in summer. The GTO might be hard on gas, but it's Hubert's most valuable car in terms of his investment. "I think that one is worth about $46,000," he says.

And his third antique is a 1972 Oldsmobile Cutlass Supreme convertible.

Also gracing his thirty- by fifty-foot garage are a 2003 sports Mitsubishi and a 2005 remodelled Mustang.

Hubert says he tinkers with his cars in winter when he tweaks that which needs tweaking and repairs anything that needs fixing. He keeps the garage heated year-round because, "You have to be careful to keep mildew from the upholstery."

Hubert considers himself fortunate to have his two daughters and a son living practically next door. Two of them are in Saulnierville and the other lives in nearby Meteghan. That was especially important to him in 2012 when his wife, Judy, passed away after a battle with cancer.

"It was good having them so close at that time," he says.

Hubert Saulnier is at the age when most men start to consider retirement, but for now, at least, retirement is not on his front burner.

CHAPTER 25

A Big Gamble Pays Off

Gilbert Simms is not the type of man you would associate with gambling. A quiet, gentle man with a genuine disarming smile, Gilbert puts you at ease within seconds of meeting him.

Ten years ago, Gilbert decided to put just about everything on the line and got into the mussel farming business in his hometown of Little Bay, located near Springdale on Newfoundland's northeast coast. You could ask what was so risky about that, but anyone who knows the aquaculture industry, especially mussel farming, will tell you that the industry was going through its darkest hour in 2004, and even established growers were going out of business.

Gilbert and his wife lived and worked in western Newfoundland at the time, and through visits back home they were aware of what was happening in the mussel industry, because there was a farm in Little Bay that was struggling to survive. Gilbert kept a close eye on things, and when the Little Bay farm was forced to close its doors, he made his move and submitted a purchase offer. Not only that, he also made offers on other farms that were going belly up. That way, he would have enough gear to start a sizable operation. LBA Enterprises was the result.

Gilbert Simms

Because mussel farms are in the ocean, a buyer is merely purchasing equipment. Water rights are not his or hers to buy or sell—you have to deal with the government for lease arrangements. So, after putting just about everything he had on the line, Gilbert Simms found himself the owner of a lot of mussel-farming gear but nothing else. Even the mussels that were on the gear in the water at the time of purchase had to be discarded because he didn't have a harvesting licence at that time. In fact, some of the gear, especially rope, was useless, too, and had to be destroyed.

Gilbert says that many of his friends were afraid he was making the biggest mistake of his life. Those local companies were going out of business because markets for Newfoundland and Labrador mussels had dried up and farmers could hardly give away product. Prince Edward Island growers were intent on market domination in Atlantic Canada, and because they were more established and had other market advantages, they were selling mussels at bargain basement prices.

However, where most people could only see an impossible business environment, Gilbert Simms saw opportunity. Gear was selling at very low prices because farmers were desperate to make anything they could salvage from their dying enterprises, and as Gilbert's good friend and mussel farmer, Lloyd Fudge from Brighton, pointed out, the industry had no place to go but up.

Knowing that it would take three long years before he would have a single pound of product to sell, Gilbert rolled up his sleeves and worked twelve to fourteen hours a day, six or seven days a week, determined to be successful. The former woodsman, who also fished crab for a couple of years in the early 1980s, was not afraid of hard work. He'd never done work at a nine-to-five job, and although his new venture would demand more work than anything he had ever done before, the satisfaction of working to grow his own business was different—it was invigorating.

Gilbert got a bit of a break in the three years that his product was growing to commercial size and quality. His instinct back in 2004 was correct and the market improved, and when his first 200,000 pounds of mussels were ready for harvest in 2007, prices had firmed up to thirty-nine cents a pound, a viable level. In fact, the price of mussels have not increased much since then. In 2012, Gilbert says he sold for forty-two cents per pound, but now that his farm has been certified as "organic," he's hoping for a higher "premium" price soon.

Since his first harvest of 200,000 pounds, Gilbert has expanded his farming area to include about 100 hectares of water surface and his harvest has increased to 1.2 million pounds in 2012. When I was there in the summer of 2013, he expected his next annual harvest would produce about the same amount.

The good news is that he has orders for every pound he can grow. Gilbert doesn't sell retail but has opted to sell to several buyers, including Juan Roberts in Triton, Green Seafoods Ltd. in Winterton, and Eveleigh's located near Twillingate.

Standing on the wharf in Little Bay with Gilbert Simms on a calm summer morning, you can't help but get caught up in his enthusiasm for the mussel-growing industry as he happily explains the ins and outs of how seed is collected, how socking is done, and how they harvest mussels in winter. He sketches drawings on a notepad to show you exactly what is happening underwater throughout the various processes.

Looking out over the beautiful pristine waters of Little Bay, one can't help but wonder what more could possibly be needed to have Gilbert's farm certified as "organic."

"It's all about your operational activities," he explains. "We have to have food-grade oil for our barges, as well as high-grade grease, and everything for all the gear, and you have to make sure there is no debris of any kind in the water that would create a negative environmental impact," he says.

"So, even if there should happen to be a small spill of anything, there would be no environmental problem."

And then there is the obligatory detailed paper trail that is required to keep the bureaucrats happy—not only for environmental reasons, but government has many demands, including traceability of product in case something goes wrong at the consumer end.

"We have to number everything. I record every detail so that, if anyone asks, I can say that this mussel came from, say, section A1, site C2, or whatever."

All that extra effort costs money, and it is certainly time-consuming, but the hope is that now that all the larger mussel growers in Newfoundland and Labrador have been certified, they will get a higher return for their product.

At fifty-seven, Gilbert has no immediate plans for retirement, but when the day comes, he figures that at least one of his two sons might be interested. They both work in Fort McMurray now but come home often and are keen to work on the farm.

"There's always something to do year-round," Gilbert says, adding that he hopes to expand to include an additional forty hectares.

"We started this business because my wife and I wanted to come back home, and so far I love the business, and while we won't get rich at it, we can make a living—and that's all we want."

Jim Wellman grew up in Port Anson, a small fishing and logging community on Newfoundland's northeast coast. The son of a schooner captain, Jim never strayed far from his marine roots despite choosing a career in journalism. For fifteen years, Jim was host of the popular radio program the Fisheries Broadcast on CBC Radio in Newfoundland. After taking an early retirement from the radio business in 1997, Jim turned off the microphone and picked up a pen. He has written six books with marine connections.

Jim has been contracted by several agencies and corporations, such as Marine Atlantic, the Canadian Sealers Association, and Heritage Canada, to draw from his marine knowledge, particularly in the fishing industry. In November 2002, Jim became managing editor of the *Navigator*, Atlantic Canada's premier fisheries and marine magazine.

INDEX